# I-94

## a collection of southwest michigan writers

there *is* something that connects us all...

# I-94

a collection of
southwest michigan
writers

edited by
brett van emst

Library of Congress Catalog Number:

ISBN: 0-9667097-0-5

photographs by brett van emst
cover design, typesetting & layout by brett van emst

"West Michigan Story" originally published
in *Holland: Volume 4* by Randall P. Vande Water.

"The Invisible Yet Incontrovertible Power of Fish"
is an excerpt from the forthcoming novel by the same name.

*additional editing by*
*kisja gunderson, trisha tartoni, and rosey cleveland*
*special thanks to kent & linda van emst*


*Manufactured in the United States of America*


first edition


## 3 a.m. publishing
east lansing • portage

**in memory of
michelle farrell**

# contents:

## fiction

## fact

# poetry

fiction

## mary blocksma

Mary Blocksma's book, *The Fourth Coast,* has brought her to the forefront in Michigan authors. Calling both Saugatuck and Beaver Island home, she shares her passion of writing with others through writing workshops. Mary's essay "Mango Child" will be featured in her next book.

## mango child

It was a mango, some say, not an apple, that dangled from the Tree of the Knowledge of Good and Evil, and a woman who first dared its enchantment.

"Oh, Adam, you must try this," Eve must have urged, rushing up to her husband, offering the gleaming peeled fruit with dripping hands, sweet juice glossing her lips. Despite the distraction from his plant nomenclature project, Adam-this being Paradise-immediately recognized the ultimate act of a loving heart, which finds more pleasure in pleasuring than in pleasure itself. Eve's eagerness to share the tree's sole fruit, to resist consuming the whole thing by herself, was surely an act of archetypal generosity. And if men proved then as hard to shop for as they seem now, Eve must have felt a particular triumph bearing her golden gift. Surely no male, however rational, remote, or overworked, could resist the spicy fragrance or tender rich flesh of a mango.

Adam ate the fruit, alternating juicy bites with his wife, and filled with ecstasy before unknown and wanting more, asked her where she had gotten it. When she told him that it was the Forbidden Fruit, their pleasure was replaced by grief, for there was not another. Thus did our ancestors learn that there is no love without loss, no ecstasy without normalcy, no enchantment without disillusionment. To eat of one is to deal with the pit of the other.

"All is not lost, my love," Eve said at last, blowing her nose in a fig leaf. If God gives you lemons, make lemonade. Let's plant that seed and grow another Tree and, with nurturing and patience, we shall again these pleasures prove."

"Good thinking!" said Adam, sucking the last sweet flecks from the pit. "There's no sauce like anticipation."

The paradox, accepted thus, proved fertile, sometimes providing mangos, or, victim of drought or neglect, sometimes not, but surviving and thriving in sunny climes to this day.

I did not benefit from this introduction to mangos. I had been taught the King James apple version, although I wasn't all that crazy about apples myself and I couldn't imagine those tempting the famous Eve. I thought of Eden's Forbidden Fruit as closely related to the poisoned apple offered by the wicked queen to Snow White, who liked apples better than I did.

A mango, however, I would have understood, for, at the age of seven, I fell under its spell as if potioned. The oldest child of a medical missionary newly sent to Lahore, Pakistan, the first time I was served the three parts of a sliced mango-two cheeks and a flat, fruit-rimmed stone-and cautiously spooned out a bite, my eyes must have popped out of my head. How could such bliss not be a sin? Dare I eat more? Oh yes, and yes again. Unlike Eve, I would not have shared.

Serving a mango to a missionary's child can prove a dangerous thing. Mangos are messy, defying conventional etiquette. I learned to delicately spoon the meat from each skin-boat, but there was always the stone, best chewed white and clean over the kitchen sink, chin dripping, fingers slippery with juice. Each pore of my nature opened to its impossible pleasure. The size and shape of my young girl's heart, sweet and pungent, with wine-like complexity, mangos reduced the sensuous landscape to safe, intoxicating mouthfuls.

I developed a hunger for perfect fruits, which, for voluptuous pleasure, have never in my life been equaled except by exquisite sex. Both give far more that I might even unreasonably expect: they go on pleasuring, on and on, so far past expectation that, attaining heaven, the notion of death seems briefly ridiculous. In that moment I live forever, and in me will that time in my life, that place, that companion, the unique shape of that moment's love and pain, be preserved in its own juice. I absorb and am absorbed by it.

So I could tell the story of my life by a history of

my encounters with perfect fruits, the time when each kind was consumed with unusual delectation: mulberries dripping from Lahore trees shrilling with drunken parrots, bulging blackberries stolen with bleeding hands from a treacherous Michigan thicket, figs consumed in a Delphi moonlight, where I was nearly raped, Nigerian papayas big as babies, wild chokecherry syrup soaking into Laramie pancakes, tangy Macintosh apples snapping in a New Hampshire orchard, navel oranges plucked daily from my northern California front porch, sweet ruby cherries missed by Michigan pickers, Hawaiian apple bananas silky as flan.

Mangos, however, remain my favorite. All my life I have searched our supermarkets for mangos to match the tenderness, intensity, and size of those preserved in my childhood memories, but have not yet found one. I have come to believe that a mango in its prime is rarely found far from the tree.

## jacqueline carey

Jacqueline Carey is from Saugatuck, Michigan. Author of a non-fiction book entitled Angels, she has had works published in *QUANTA*, *The Open Scroll*, and was nominated for *eSCENE: The world's best online fiction.* "Jazznight" is set during the Saugatuck Jazz Festival and chronicles a young boy's first glimpse into an adult world.

*jazznight*

When it gets dark the town turns on all its Christmas lights- all the twinkling lights strung in the trees
along the sidewalks, plus all the light shining off the
bright metal and glass in the ice cream stores and
coffee shops, all the neon shouting from the windows
of the bars. Only it doesn't look like Christmas
because it's summer and it's warm and all the trees
have leaves. It looks like fairyland.

Fairyland, fairyland, he sings soundlessly to himself, only shaping the words. His father looks down
and grins. "Doing okay, pal? Not tired?" He shakes
his head no, no, not tired, then keeps shaking it,
making himself delirious and dizzy. His father laughs
and puts a hand on his head to still him.

All over town, there is music. The fairy lit night

dances with it.  All over town people are humming
and singing, smiling like his father.  The doors of the
crowded, laughing bars stand open and music floods
out and, ticklish and dancing, follows them down the
street like a stray cat.  He laughs out loud.

"See?  He likes it."

His mother says nothing, so he knows she is angry,
but she reaches down and squeezes his hand so he
knows it isn't at him.

Earlier he knew she was angry when she slammed
down the telephone and yelled at his father, "There
isn't a god damn baby sitter free in the whole
goddamn town tonight!"  And then, "We should have
gone last night.  You knew my sister would have
watched him last night," and her voice was bitter.
And his father; "Never mind, honey.  We'll take him
with us."

It had gone on for a long time that time and he
had pretended not to hear.  "Oh,  for god's sake, Joe,
he's only six."  "He's old enough.  He stayed up for
New Year's. Remember?  We won't stay late."  And on
and on and he pretended not to hear until his father
came into the den all smiles and said, "Hey pal, I
want you to do me a big favor.  Can you take an
extra-long nap for me?  Can you do that?"

He could, he did, he had, because even though he
pretended not to hear, he knew what it meant, so he
had.  Now, he is wide awake as they walk along the
docks.

"It's so pretty at night," his mother says, forgetting
to be mad.

The water is black because it's night, but all the

lights of the boats and the bars sparkle on its surface, rippling and dancing.  In the middle of the harbor a boat sounds its horn, a long, blaring blast that makes the dock shiver under the soles of their feet.

"Oh look'" his mother says, and points at the hand-cranked chain ferry, boarding noisy, laughing passengers at the end of the dock.  The ferry is made of white curlicues like icing on a wedding cake and twinkling all over tonight with strings of Christmas lights.  On the far side of the river another bar beckons, wafting bright music across the water.  "We should ride the ferry, Joe." "Maybe later."  His father looks across the river then looks at his watch, and begins to steer them from the dock.  "I told Mark we'd meet them at Wally's at ten and it's already five after."

Away from the river they go, cutting through the little park with its dark huddled bushes, past the shadowy lattices of the bandstand where two people clutch and sigh at each other, back to the lively streets and lights and people and he can see their faces again.

Even from the sidewalk the patio of Wally's Bar and Grill is crowded,  people sitting at all the tables and leaning against the picket fence, even though the music from inside is muted outside.  His father takes the lead, striding ahead, greeting friends who shout his name, making a path.  Suddenly overcome, he clings to his mother's hand as they follow his father into the dark mouth of the bar.  Inside it is dark and crowded and full of jazz.

"Joe!" someone shouts from a table at the back of the bar, right in front of the band.  His father plunges into the thick of the crowd, cuts through people like a strong swimmer. His mother follows in his wake and he clutches a fold of her skirt, winding through a crush of strange legs, clinging to her.

And then they reach the table, all of them, and people are changing seats, shifting and making room, and his father sits down and puts him on his lap and he is out of the forest, able to see again.

"How's that, pal?"

He wriggles in response, bounces to the music. There are three men in the band because it is a small bar and there isn't much room. One plays drums, one plays cello and one plays a guitar. They're all sweating. The man playing guitar, perched on a stool, is close enough for him to touch if he leaned way forward.

The guitar player is a black man. He's never seen a black man up close before.

Conversation flows around and above him. Even when he listens hard at times like this he cannot understand what they are saying -his mother and his father and their friends.

"...and the Pope says, I'm sorry, Dopey, my son, but I know every order in the Catholic Church and there are no dwarf nuns," his father's friend Mark Philbrook is saying. "So the other six dwarfs go, ah, Dopey, we told you so! You fucked a penguin!"

Everyone laughs. He watches the musicians. They don't look at anyone or anything, not even each other. When he watches them, the conversation at the table blurs and all he can hear is the music. The drummer is using brushes instead of drumsticks. Swish, he whispers without a sound, swish swish. The drummer's head bobs like there's a spring hidden inside him.

When the waitress finally squeezes through to their table, his mother says it's okay if he has a Coke. It has more fizz than regular Coke from a can. He drinks it too fast at first and then drinks only in tiny slurps to make it last, kicking his heels against the rungs of his father's chair.

After a while, the band takes a break. Everyone in the bar claps. When the band stops, all their voices suddenly seem loud without the music. Then one of the bartenders puts some music on the stereo and the river of voices flows smoothly again.

The three men from the band sit at the table next to theirs, greeting friends. He feels shy of them and looks the other way. Some people are leaving the bar now that the band isn't playing. It is easier to see the people sitting at the other tables.

A pretty lady in a hat sees him looking and smiles. He hides his face in his father's shoulder.

"Whassamatter, pal?" his father asks. "You gettin' tired?"

Face still buried, he shakes his head, rubbing his nose and cheeks against the soft faded cotton of his father's shirt until his skin tingles. His father laughs, hoists him up. Then sets him down on his feet and ruffles his hair. "Go on to your mom for a while, huh?"

His mother is talking to Mark Philbrook's girl-friend. Their heads are leaned together and their voices are low and sharp. He tugs on her sleeve once.

"Not now, punkin," she says. He looks at his father but his father is laughing hard at something Mark has said, his head thrown back. The waitress brings another round of beer but no Coke for him this time. No one is watching, so he inches his way around the table, hanging on to the back of his mother's chair.

Now he is beside the musicians' table. They're quieter than his mother and father and their friends, talking easily. A black woman's sitting by the guitar player is holding a little girl on her lap; younger than him, almost a baby. The little girl's skin is lighter than the woman's or the guitar player's. His mother drinks coffee with a lot of milk in it every morning. The little girl's skin is that color.

His father's other friend, Dave, is talking to the man who played the big cello. Now the cello-man stands up and Dave stands up and they shake hands. All the musicians and their friends and their family stand up. He shrinks back against the edge of the table as they squeeze past, him between the two tables.

"Careful." Dave puts a big hand on his shoulder and draws him out of the way, back by his own chair. He smiles up at Dave; way up, because Dave is very tall. Dave sits down again and smiles back at him. He used to be scared of Dave, when he was little, because Dave is so big and has a big bushy beard that makes him look like a bear-man, but he isn't anymore.

Some loud people are pushing their way through to the musicians' empty table. "Come here, punkin," his mother says. "Let these people get past," even though he isn't in their way.

"So how old is he now?" Mark Philbrook's girlfriend asks his mother. "Five or six?" He knows her name but doesn't like her so he forgets it. Her face is too pinched and her voice is screechy. "Screech-Owl" his father calls her when Mark isn't there.

"Six last March," says his mother. "He starts first grade in the fall, don't you?"

He nods. Mark's girlfriend smiles with her pinched mouth. She wears a lot of lipstick and it's smeared in the corners of her lips, like she has a bloody mouth. Dave is talking to Mark now, so he can't go back there. He ducks under the table and squirms past his mother's knees emerging next to his father.

"Hiya, pal!" His father's voice sounds loose and slurry. "Hop up." He clambers back onto his father's lap. The air is full of smoke from all the people in the bar smoking cigarettes. He starts to feel sleepy, then maybe does fall asleep for a while, because when he opens his eyes again the band has come back without their families and the are tuning up their instruments.

The music begins again and he is too sleepy now to feel like bouncing or dancing, but the music goes in him, deeper than before, echoing in the hollow space inside his chest. In his head the jazz still dances while his heart beats to the steady throm-throm-thrump sound of the big cello. This is true nighttime, the secret world of grown-ups.

Everyone in the bar looks vague and soft from the fog of beer and jazz and smoke, except for the musicians, who look more like themselves. The guitar player plays with his eyes closed. Sweat shines on his black face under the little spotlight. His square fingernails are a pale pink color against the dark skin of his quick-moving fingers.

It's comfortable in the curve of his father's arms. If he lays his head down, his father's voice rumbles in his right ear beneath the sound of the music all around them. Wrapped in warmth and music, he slides in and out of wakefulness and then, finally falls, falls down the long dark tunnel of sleep. For a long time the music follows him down, then it too fades in the soft darkness.

He slowly wakes up when his father shakes him but not all the way. It's late, very late, and the band is taking their last break of the night.

"Time to go home, pal," his father says, sounding cheerful. Everything is blurred with sleep. He stumbles when his father sets him down. His mother catches his hand and steadies him, says good-night to their friends. Dave smiles at him, but he's too tired to smile back. His father says good-night too, takes his wallet from his back pocket and counts out some money, leaving it on the table to pay.

They ease their way out of the bar, through the people standing and drinking and talking. Outside it's a little cooler than it was and the patio is half-empty, but they can't leave because the man who sits at the gate and looks at people's driver's licenses is blocking the way and a drunk woman is yelling at him. "I'm sorry," the man at the gate says to her without moving. "You'll have to leave."

"Do you know how much money I spend here?" asks the drunk woman, loudly, weaving on her feet and her eyes not quite right. She looks mean. "Huh?

D' you know how much fuckin' money?"

"Too much," says someone at one of the tables and a spatter of laughter circles the patio. The drunk women glares and shouts something but the trolley that is for special occasions comes down the street right then with all its lights twinkling and a group of new people come off it making noise and laughing and no one hears what the drunk lady says.

"Fuck you," she says as the man at the gate moves her out of the way to let the new people through. "Fuck you!" As the new people file through the gate, she fumbles with her bicycle that is leaning against the fence and rides off, wobbling slowly down the street.

The man at the gate shakes his head. "An accident waiting to happen," he says. The trolley dings its bell and pulls away from the curb, headed for the next bar. "'Night, folks," says the man at the gate as they leave.

He stays close to his mother and father both as they cross the street, so they have to walk together with him. Behind them the trolley rounds the corner and disappears. Ahead of them the drunk lady on the bicycle weaves and swears. His father hums a little song. A soft breeze carries a strain of music from another bar and the drunk lady's curses, rustling the leaves in the trees and making the fairy-lights dance.

A solitary car is coming down the main street, approaching them at a right angle. In slow motion, wobbling and weaving and swearing, the drunk lady rides her bicycle right through the stop sign.

Tires squeal and metal crunches; everything is sudden and fast and shocking and he sees the bike caught under the car's front tires, sees the drunk lady fly, sees her head strike the pavement. His mother is screaming a high thin scream that goes on and on, and then his father jerks him into a rough embrace, crushing his face against his cotton shirt.

Unable to see, he clings blindly to his father. People run past them shouting and in the distance, sirens begin to wail. He is shaking. When his father lets him lift his head, people are crowded around the drunk lady, their shadows long and black before the headlights of the stopped car. A police car pulls up, staining all the people in washes of red and blue light.

His mother has stopped screaming; she stoops and holds his face, strokes his hair, saying, "It's okay, sweetheart, everything's okay, Daddy's going to take us home now."

Her voice is too high and her face is strange in the headlights and police lights. He doesn't mean to, but he starts to cry. His father carries him and covers his eyes, even though he knows from the voices and the sounds and the police radios that they are passing the accident, and then it fades a little and a car door opens and his father puts him in the back seat.

In the car the engine is running and they are driving away and in the back seat he falls asleep and dreams, he dreams of fairy lights and black men with dancing fingers and tires screaming, cigarette smoke and drumbrush and throm-throm cello heartbeat, dark wetness shining on the pavement and bicycles and jazz music bright light light light and the drunk lady flying through the air.

## tom short

Tom Short, of Portage, has spent the majority of his life fishing and writing in Montana. He is enrolled in the University of Montana's Writing Program. "At the Drive Thru", a story he wrote while in Michigan, portrays a lost sense of place. The work is a glimpse into the younger generations views of love. Look for his first novel sometime in 1999.

## *at the drive thru*

"What do you do to be a tough guy?" I ask Chris because he used to be a tough guy before he cut his hair and started walking around our parties picking up Bud Light bottles before we can throw them off the fire escape. When he was a tough guy he was known for walking around the very same parties and biting the tops of beer cans off and just letting his lip bleed all over the dance floor.

"What do you mean?" Chris asked. We're in his Lincoln trying to find some fast food that's still open, preferably a Wendy's, Chris wants a Frosty.

"I mean that tough guy image. You used to have

it."

"Well, the thing is you gotta act like there's something more important than whatever you're doing at the moment."

"That seems like being a jerk." I say. I'm playing with the power seats.

"It's a thin line, I'll grant ya." Chris is smoking a cigarette. The weather is shitty out and freezing. It's always like this in February in Michigan. "The difference is the fact that you do have something that's more important, not just that you don't care."

The smoke from his cigarette is being sucked out the smoker's window and we see a BK and pull into the drive thru. I can feel the Jack Daniels burning in my stomach.

"You want to know a sure fire way to get a girl?" he says while he's putting down his power window. "What do you want?"

"Whopper meal, go large." And then I think about that mad cow stuff I saw on TV. "No, get me the chicken combo."

I look at the chicken combo on the sign and it looks like shit and decide to take my chances, "No, get me the whopper meal with a Coke. How do you?"

"Hang on." Chris gives the guy our order. He only gets a vanilla shake.

"Okay, I'm at this party one time last year, only I'm hitting it with Rachel at the time and she calls me up and says she's coming over. I mean, what do I care? I've been doing my laundry all night walking around in sweats and a T-shirt." He takes a drag on the cigarette and puts his window down to pay. Our total is $6.11. The damn shake was $2.10.

"So," he says getting the change from the guy, "I'm downstairs getting my laundry out of the dryers and there are people partying all around. The DJ's blasting in the room next to the laundry room. Thanks." He takes the food from the guy and starts putting up his window. "Make sure that fucker gave us everything." I look through the bag and everything's there.

"Well, on my way out with my laundry, this girl asks me why I'm not partying and I tell her that I'm tired. Ya know, that I had things to do. And she's like 'C'mon and dance with me, please' and this girl and I start talking and hit it off right away. She was from the U.P. and likes to deer hunt and shit like that."

Then he's silent.

I look around outside and the town is icy as shit with the rain during the day and the freezing at night. I look at him and say, "So that's the story? Did Rachel come?"

"Yeah, and that was it, but I *could* have hit it with this girl simply because when I met her, I wasn't *trying* to hit it with anyone. I didn't care. I had something else on my mind." He takes another drag on his cigarette.

"Your laundry?"

"My laundry."

And then he thinks about it.

"I should have gotten her phone number at least, but that's the way to get some lovin'," and he says this last word like a phone sex girl.

"God, love?  I haven't been in love for four years."
I say that because my old girlfriend's been on my
mind a lot lately.

"You were in love once?"

"Well, the closest I've ever been, I guess."  I say.
We are taking the long way back to the fraternity
house.  There aren't many cars out on the road.
Everything is quiet in town.

"With who?"

"My girlfriend from high school."

"What?"

"She was incredible, she really was."  And I pause.
"We were inseparable for a while.  We did everything
together."  And I try to remember her, to picture her
face, a smile or a laugh or the ways she says certain
words, but I can't.  I can't remember her face at all.
All I can picture is the beautiful hair she had.  She had
the most incredible hair.

Chris laughs and then he throws his cigarette butt
out the smoker's window.

"Do you ever talk to her now?"  He asks.

"No.  Not for a long time.  She's got a boyfriend
now."

We're pulling into the driveway and the mainhouse
is dead black.  Chris grabs his movie from the back
seat and we roll into the house with our food.

Walking in Chris says, "So that was your true love,
huh?"

"Hell," I say.  "I thought so."  And I did, and, at
times, I still do.

We sit down in the living room which my bedroom door opens to.  I set my sack with my Burger

King on the coffee table and flip on the TV. I have to clean a spot by moving empty beer cans and dip cups and other Burger King bags which are spotted gray with week-old ketchup stains.

"What ever happened between you and Rachel?" I ask. I'm unwrapping my burger.

"Well," He lights up another cigarette and pulls a Slurpee cup close to him for an ash tray. "She got annoying."

He says this and seems satisfied that this statement sums up two months of sleeping together, traveling together, studying together, and hanging out talking, and then, one morning, waking up and finding her annoying. "Can I throw the movie in?"

I nod because my mouth is full of Whopper. It tastes a lot better then the Chicken sandwich looked.

He gets up and puts the movie in.

"You got to move on quickly. Never let it seem like you want to be with them." He is back in his advice giving mode now, and I am more than happy to listen. Everyone can talk the game but he, he was respected because he knew it. He knew the game like his own face and he had perfected it, and I, I who had been coming up short for a while longer then I would like to admit, was willing to listen to find something there.

"Get it so she stops by. Then you got it made. You go study for a couple hours, come home, and she is there or go to the bar with your friends and she's there with hers and you both know that she is to stop by at two-thirty or so, and crawl into bed with you. That's when it's the best."

I think about my girlfriend and how her parents had caught her in a lie once when she had spent the night at my house when my parents were gone. She got in trouble for that, but I could still go see her at her house. When I showed up for the first time after she got in trouble, her dad told me he had a shotgun. He was joking, of course, and I knew it but it made my girlfriend mad but he just laughed and laughed. I laughed to but didn't think we were the good friends he thought we were, as if it wasn't his doing -it was his wife who had grounded my girlfriend, not him.

I used to tell my girlfriend I loved her. I told her that all the time. And still, she is the only one I have ever said that to. That day, when I went to see her when she was in trouble with her parents, I accidentally told her I loved her when her dad was in the room and he must have heard. That was something I never did. And I was scared because I knew I meant it, and I thought that would scare him, or me, but he didn't even look up from what he was reading. He didn't even seem concerned.

"College is a one time thing." Chris says eyeing what's left of his cigarette. "I'll be damned if I'm going to spend time and money with one girl when this is the last time I can do this sort of shit."

And Chris takes a big pull off of his cigarette.

"I mean, shit, in two years I won't be able to do this sort of thing and won't want to." Chris is eating my fries and I realize that the movie is starting.

"What movie is this?"

"Some old western starring Eastwood. Listen, it comes down to this. It would be perfect if you could just swing by some girl's house on your way home from the bar or have her there waiting for you. You still do things together but only when you want to."

"A Drive Thru?"

"Shit, why not?"

And I'm still picturing my girlfriend's dad looking down and not looking up even though he must have heard. I know he must have heard. And I can barely see my old girlfriend's face now, just her long hair, that incredible hair, but I can picture him there looking down reading as clear as I can see Chris here, now. I can see he thinks it is all nothing.

I look back to the TV, smell the hanging smoke from the tough guy's cigarette, and try my hardest to remember what my girlfriend's face looked like.

## kim gehrke

Kim Gehrke has been freelance
writing for the last ten years. She has
had stories and articles published in
*Michigan-Out-of-Doors* and *The Grand
Haven Tribune.* The excerpt "The
Invisible Yet Incontrovertible Power of
Fish" is from her second novel (same
title) which will soon be published.
The story is as "Michigan" as it can
get, encountering memories of a
michigan upbringing at every turn.

*the invisible yet incontrovertible power of fish*

I parked the car on the side of the abandoned road
and got out, pushing the station wagon's heavy door
shut behind me. Its closing rang out an invading
metallic sound that reverberated like a shot fired into
the chamber of barren trees, of blank meadow, of
hollow air. I could feel its echo moving away from me
slowly, endless as concentric circles widening on water
broken by a rock. Maybe it was because there was no
other sound here that I perceived their invading effect
-nothing but an eerily-reposed forest which exhaled
out, leafless and sodden for more than twenty miles all
around. It was a landscape quiet as a pond's smooth
surface with no ripples, no depth. It was a mirror of
trees with no reflection of me.

My keys dropped from my hand into the dirt at

my feet, as my dog, who heeled at my side, lowered her head to sniff them, then looked up at me. It is uncanny how dogs could stare right into your eyes and read you. Mine looked at me with an expression of bewilderment. She wanted to run and she seemed to wonder why we didn't just begin, why I would even question the impulse. I unzipped my anorak and pushed it from my shoulders, letting it's cool nylon fabric slide down my arms to hang from the snapped cuffs at my wrists. The three delicate petals of trillium, spring's first flower, lifted up from the muddy forest floor before me, bowing bright green and white amidst the gray grove of popple. They were so white and so close to the ground I could have mistaken them for the snow which still lingered here and there. There was a solace in looking at them. They were sighs of kindness in the face of winter's stoic pall. I pulled the jacket sloppily, impatiently from my wrists. The sun had broken through and I was warm.

I stared out into the mottled ranks of white birch, maple and oak. They were so imperturbable and silent -no birds, nothing -that I couldn't believe that anything lived there. They were as unsoundable an expanse as Lake Michigan's rough, cold horizon, stretching out to limits dwarfing my senses and swelling with dormant trees, their life still shrouded within by chill wave upon wave of wet bark. I stood upon the dry bank of road and felt them rolling in on me. They fell like sheets of water upon fire, like enveloping curtains of their own heavy breath upon my breath. A swell of wind suddenly heaved itself over and through them and the trillium trembled,

their white flowers quaking like surf retreating down
the shore;  its sound was the same slow watery thunder of waves that I dared fall asleep to when I lived on
the shore of the great lake, its low-pitched visceral
rumble recollecting memories of the darkness of that
little house and the roar of stormy breakers all night,
crashing upon the nearby stone beaches.  Night was
their time, when you were unable to ignore them;
there was nothing then to distract you -no traffic, no
hum of the city -save TV, and when you clicked it off
late in the evening, its light receding into the tube and
leaving you alone, you sometimes needed a drink to
sleep.  It was incredible -the roar of that surf was the
same heavy rolling that I was hearing now, and yet I
was a hundred miles away from its shore.  And there
wasn't any house or rocky beach here.  There was only
this isthmus of road.  The willowy tips of a stand of
pine beside it began to pitch and roll in the force
pressing down on them.  I was beneath it, in the
calmness of the breaker, and it was surging above me.
It's gathering force eddied around me, churning
branches with brittle cracks and grating, timber
twisting screaks.  Suddenly it was gone, moved on,
still as breath.  It had pushed over me without a
thought.

Unlike in Lake Michigan's icy waters, if I took off
all my clothes now and waded in above my head, I
wouldn't drown.  I would immerse myself in this
breathable sea of woods, into its living river of
memory, without one desperate gulp of air.  It was
different from the lake where, when you stood looking into the water from above, all you ever saw was

you, your reflection curiously looking back. Looking under its surface-that was another matter. You disappeared into the murky depths; there was no image of you looking back anymore. You strained to see anything. Most of your senses weren't any good to you at all. You had to rely on, develop others if you were going to live. You open your mouth and it fills with water. Suddenly your swimming strongly, constantly, buoyed along by the singular need to survive. You're quiet and waiting for anything, anything new, unordinary that may teach you how to live, no matter how foggily discerned, how foolishly commanding. My hand was at the neck of my shirt, unbuttoning. It could overtake you like that, without you even perceiving its slow inundation. I watched detached as it moved down the placket, undoing one button at a time. Suddenly your in the tall swells, struggling for your life, struggling to keep from going under only by learning to command the strokes. I stopped to reflect: what would the next improbable traveler down this logging road think, finding abandoned here a heap of clothes, a car, keys in the dirt.

My shoulder slipped out from beneath my sweater and the sun touched it for the first time in months; the breeze was light and warm upon it like a stranger's breath exhaled from behind. To slip in, under, begin swimming -it would be as easy as taking off one's clothes. Just drop them, wade in and make off at a steady stroke toward the blue-green horizon of the ocean, or even Lake Michigan. There were fish five feet long that swam in those dark, cold tides, living prehistoric existences with narrow, gnashing teeth, flipping fin or tail out above the surface only during the boiling pot of mating and thus suggesting that they did indeed exist. Then they would show you only glimpses of their curious and shining bodies with glee, leaving you to wonder about the rest. You could stare at the flat and turbid lake for seasons, watching it roll in winter and lay flaccid in summer, and never be able to imagine what went on beneath its waves.

That is, until you pulled a fish out. Lifting a big, fat, gasping Brown Trout out of its shadow-darting greenness, you'd have to hold it with two hands deep in its flexing gills -it slapping them against your wrist in an attempt to breathe while it wrestled for its life with you -and still not believe the strangeness and wonder of the creature. It would require all your strength just to hold it up, while its blood ran winding paths from its very innards, from its open wound of gills down your bare arms. It would be a long time before you got over that -its eyes red and glaring with their last moments of vision, while it hissed at you. You'd even be dreaming about it for months: flopping about hard on the concrete of the pier, smashing scales and guts from its ripped up mouth on the pavement. Maybe that's why fisherman in Michigan spent half a fortune and half a lifetime in pursuit of Muskie. It was an obsession for them. It was something they needed to know, that kind of special knowing which came only from experiencing the previously unfathomable. It was true that you could never really guess how you would act in an unmanageable situation until you were in one. When you pulled a thing that mean and big out of the deep, a creature that was equally willing to devour you as you were it, to wrestle it into the boat as it tried to take a piece of your hand with its vicious mouthful of meat-eating teeth, then you definitely had a trophy. I mean, that was some kind of contest. I suppose then you truly knew something important about what went on in those filmy reaches. At least, after having met it face-to-face, you'd have a pretty good clue.

A lone White-tail Deer leapt across the narrow tree-couched lane, far down where its descending line was shrouded in shadow. It happened only an instant after I turned, bounding out of the guts of living woods across this scar of road, this leaping point of us to them. The experience had its own resonance which was memory of the sight playing over and over again in my mind as I held my breath. I saw the deer bounding. I remembered its bounding, its legs folded up inward beneath it as if, for that moment, it was the center of all the forest which unfolded in all directions from that one point. But I was wrong. Every sparrow was counted in these anonymous woods.

I was given a glimpse of what awaited me down at the end of the road. I was going down it alone, into where it disappeared into darker, untouched stands. Its long stretch of graded dirt moved beneath my feet as I walked; turned soft by spring thaw, its abandoned length was now impassable by car. The water perco-lating from below had slid whole sections of it into the drainage ditches on either side. Melting frost bled steadily from holes in the earth, coalescing into cleansing streams which carved out its elevated sand and gravel bank. Where I was going no one else had been for months, probably years. I turned to look behind me. My car was no longer in sight. The horizon with its path out was closed off by somber, lifeless forest.

The trees here seemed so much bigger, so much taller than I had ever seen them. They competed in growth as crowded pillars barreling toward the sky. They swayed and groaned as one living, breathing being in the wind. Hissing creaks erupted within where the huge upper limbs were tossed off earthward, where whole weaker popples succumbed to the strangulation of the dominating hardwoods, throwing their weight into the crooks of oaks to bear for centuries. Yet it was still down where I was; nothing penetrated. It wasn't my life that dominated here; I was suddenly inconsequentially small, even to myself.

I thought about the moment the deer leapt. Where was it running? Why was it running alone with such deliberate purpose? Deer were always doing that to you, bolting straight out before you at heart stopping speeds. They're invisible then, BAM, they're crashing through the undergrowth with big racks, waiting until you're almost upon them to lurch. Then they always rush broadside right before you instead of hightailing it away, giving you a close but fleeting look-at their horns, powerful flanks, into their brown eyes engorged by the utter excitation of your advantageous meeting in their untraversed domain -as if it were necessary for them to be seen by you. I don't know why they did it, acting like it was their mission to flash you their speed, flexing their deftness at sailing through the ruins of fallen boughs and running on out at you with a shock, leaving you trembling, your pulse racing, your heart beating in your throat, springing a mixture of awe and adrenaline on you that left you enrapt, charged, thinking about it for a long time afterwards. People died of it: Buck Fever. Old and young men alike were keeling over from it every fall, dying alone in the woods from heart attacks, their poised and ready guns instead falling from their hands onto the rotting leaves.

I knew I had walked at least a full mile. I looked at my wrist out of habit, though I had deliberately not brought a watch along with me here. My dog was still at my heel, sentinel-like, quivering. She wanted to run. She was begging me to let her run with imploring eyes, her nose wandering across beckoning scents upon the ground with every step. She was a pitch-black mutt of Labrador mix that I had inherited only weeks before; passed along to numerous reluctant owners, it had become apparent to me that somewhere along the line someone had beat strict commands into her with a broom. They were commands she never veered from. She would remain rigidly at my side for hours as I walked, slowing if I did or responsively picking up the pace. I noticed one day that casually picking up a stick sent shivers of fear through her crouched and cowering body. She was obviously raised in terror, and I'm sure she thought that with me she'd found herself dead and gone to heaven. Named Shadow, her coat was dull and shabby from just having a load of pups, and though she barely knew me she looked up to me, head up, tail wagging, with intoxicated, unbelieving gratitude.

There it was. From here I could only see its side. It looked off alone into thirty unbroken miles of hermetic, tree-ripped landscape where no man lived. It was an outpost of waiting. It was the lonliest place I had ever seen. It was perched upon the outermost limit of what I knew, what almost anyone knew. For thirty miles to its south lay morass, virgin hemlock, hillocks of sumac and no trails; it was a preserve of impossibly true wilderness, untrammeled, insular, arcane.

Branches shook and howled ratchety creaks in the wind above. There was no softness yet from stirring leaves. It was only wind cornering the hardness of precarious and gangly limbs and the trees groaning their pained response. It was too choked with their trunks here even for a trillium to grow. There was nothing green.

I leapt the ditch on the side of the abandoned logging trail. It was filled with brackish liquid, brown with tannin distilled from tree roots. It was the blood of the soil of Michigan. Up here, huge foaming rivers ran deep with it. The mighty Grand River ripped across the state, disgorging the northern forest tree by tree, gurgling with their root sap; its flow was more tree than water, and when you sank your feet into it to wade they were gone, even in only six inches of the browness. Because of tannin the rivers' waters were always tepid, soft, their banks sand-bottomed, and when you swam they pushed against you in heavy, velvety currents that pulsed over your shoulders, embracing you in the sun. They held you quietly spellbound while veiled fish made invisible sucking forays at your ankles and toes.

I forded into the tangles of white birch. Someone else had made this trek before, that was for sure, but now the path from their steps was all but obliterated. I kept my eyes before me, upon my destination which was only slowly revealed through the clotted field of thick trunks, tripping, almost sprawling on roots that broke up through the ground. I couldn't take my eyes off the cabin as I approached. Its steep, peaked roof was an anomaly here, an intriguing curiosity which drew you in. On its side I saw there were two widows, one big and high, the other small and on the lower right corner, which were absolutely blank with darkness within; with them it seemed to be only glimpsing at me with two vacant eyes. It reserved its stare for that which lay before it, looking out from a visage which I couldn't yet see, nor surmise.

I stopped, then came up from its flank slowly, studying its thick, vertical planks of cedar siding, still red-hued beneath the eaves and worn silver-gray where the rain had streaked them below. The roof was cedar shake, in places dark with rot and caked with moss. It hung precipitously over a raised porch of pine boards, supported by four narrow posts at its outer edge, with the blackened fronds of last year's ferns crowding right up next to its floor, colonizing every foot with their own obliterating aggrandizement; the cabin was a precarious island of planed wood -a float -imperiled by the unsatiated appetite of this green world to reclaim by destruction. There was no pleasant wading from its porch. You stepped right down into the vast cold tides. Above, the spindly

crowns of white birch and maple had filled up the sky,
breathing in the light left from its construction
clearing as fast and completely as fire sucked air. It
occurred to me that if one looked from above, upon
the surface of this sea of trees, one would never
surmise what waited below.

I walked around to the front and saw two windows
on opposing sides, one small and paned, one large,
dense and opaque as ebony. They were as black and
ostensibly bottomless as the dark liquor in the ditches
beside the road: no light ever filtered down to those
and what lived there lived impervious to me amongst
the rotting leaves -the slimy, algae-devoured leaves
becoming earth. I stood in front of the large window
and it looked through me. I couldn't perturb its
quiet, restful stare. It was as content and undisturbed
in its purpose as a sealed grave.

Was I really going to live here? Was I really going
to surrender to sleep in there, and what would I find
waiting beside me when I woke up? What would I
see through that window which stared out as if in a
trance and what spell would it cast on me? I remembered diving in the cold currents of Lake Michigan.
My ears filled with water, and there was a different
kind of sound. It was a frequency that I perceived; a
high-pitched whine. I thought about how all color
was slower or faster wavelengths of light. Was I just
grappling to keep myself from drowning in this
dulling, lethargic drone of brown? I was so uneasily
alone already. There was just dampness, brown earth,
brown leaves, brown bark as far as I could see. I felt
like I had in a nightmare where I had given up my

humanity to become a fish.  But I was neither human nor a fish wholly.  I swam in an alien, unbreathable world, doomed all the while -every moment -to know that I did.

I cast out my arms and pulled myself up with both hands ahold of a square column onto the dry, pine-planked porch.  I looked at the door.  It too was rough and weathered planks of cedar.  There was a dulled, brass doorknob and a hasp without a lock.  It was never locked.  It waited, a mile deep in this forgotten timber, for anyone to climb its tall porch, duck its cedar-shake roof line and push open its portal.  It was excacting, though.  You had to walk its singular, deteriorating avenue in; the woods were impenetrable with crowded saplings that tore your skin and slapped welts upon your face, twisting themselves into your hair.  That is, except for the deer trails, which never went anywhere you wanted to go.  They never went anywhere useful to you.  I followed one once until it disappeared behind a discreet blind of cattail and sedge-into a swamp.  That was where all the unseen mysteries of nature transpired, behind that curtain of rushes where water waited, rich, teeming, inviolate.  The more water, the more rich diversity of life was creating itself.  It was from the swamps edge that the coyotes yipped out in hungry packs at night.  It was where the deer hid from all the hunters in the fall.  All deer trails were like that.  Eventually falling off hard earth into stewing marshes, where the markers were discernible to only those who lived in an unimaginably rich olfactory world.  Either that, or they seemed simply to lift off from the earth.

Michigan was deep with water, where it was carved
out and leveled by glaciers. The soil was black from
the moisture's incessant rot. Water devoured everything; it was the first and would be the last element.
It swallowed fire with a heavy, airless gulp. It hung in
the air and blew over ripe fields smelling more like the
breeze off the distant Great lakes than the hay.
Twenty, thirty, forty square miles of hardwoods
languished everywhere in soil steaming, trickling,
debauching pools of murky tinctures all over the state.
The submerged trunks of oaks as well as popple
competed in bolting growth against the fungi, decay,
mildew and putrefaction of still and stagnant mias-
mas. You could look out at these waveless, gloomy
swamps from the few avenues that dared get close to
them and frown. They would never belong to you or
anyone else. They were a world unto themselves. It
was possible that no man had ever penetrated them.
Water was, there, still creating the earth.

The cabin was perched on a fragile shelf of land at
the edge of such a swamp. You could swing at the soil
with a sledgehammer, landing it with a shaking thud,
and the water would darkly ooze out like blood. Only
the trees held it pinned down, secured it from going
under. Otherwise it would surely slip off in plates,
giving way in fissures like the road did. This place
was being forgotten. It was getting harder and harder
to walk its path back. Now you had to walk your
possessions down the mile distance in many silent
trips lasting the whole day. There would be nothing
to do but contemplate the imposing presence of
leafless trees, reaching out all around in a sleeping,

unstirring expanse. It weighed on me now as if I had walked that mile progressing deeper and deeper underground. I felt suffocated by the weight of all that earth upon me; it was insufferably mute as only the impacted, dull soil could be. I was surprised by the sound of my breath. It reminded me once more of diving where every inhalation was amplified through your gear, stringing you along from the surface to the bottom in measured paces. It was the one thing about you which you could never give over to that alien world. Its sound was the one thing that reminded you that you were inexorably separate.

I was still looking at the door. How long had I stood there? Everything was steeped in so much reflection. I wasn't buried in the ground; I was buried in me. It wasn't really mute here. My consciousness was completely consumed by my senses. There was nothing left of me besides my total concentration on what was coming into me: the slant of the light through the smooth, gray popple trunks; the cold wetness of melting frost percolating through the earth which had seeped into my shoes; the signal of a twig snapping invisibly against the ground through the brush ahead. I realized that things were affecting me which I couldn't explain. All I could do now was listen; understanding was still a distant proposition. With the listening I was inextricably living only the present. The senses fed me feelings, inundating impressions which were distinctly not mine, but were my experience of the variables of influence drifting all around me. The demand for concentration was total, and yet it was a relief. It was like being a child again

and laying your head against the breast of your
mother without a care, her hand in your hair.  It was
your all-consuming experience of her which envel-
oped and bathed you.  Not you.

   Thinking I saw something I turned around,
leaning into the door and looking out from under the
porch.  A spell of sensation had surrounded me like a
wave and was beginning to retreat, draw out with a
scattering pull of surf racing back down the shore.  I
was sitting now, leveled, back against the door, legs
flat out before me, acutely aware of the warm pine
planks of the porch.  I remembered oil drum rafts in
summer bobbing out on sparkling lakes.  I would
swim out to them calmly in the quieted swells of the
evening.  It seemed the water was the more comfortable element, the natural one, when I pulled myself
up the slippery ladder into the chill of the air.  Your
first steps were always uncertain, woozy until you
knocked the water out of your ears, and you sat down
quickly so as not to pitch yourself off its rocking
platform.  Then you would stretch out and contemplate the shore, feeling so removed.  It was a place new
and utterly unconnected to your past for, after all, you
had to swim to get there, just like a convict who,
pursued by dogs, fords a stream to erase any clues of
his presence, arriving fresh upon the opposing bank
released of his own history.  On hot summer nights I
waited until the very last rays of sunlight departed,
when the cicadas pulsed invisibly in the leafy fragrant
branches, and the blue screens of televisions illuminated the constellation of houses perched in a distant
circle around the shore's edge, before I was forced to

swim back leisurely in the calmness that mirrored the darkening sky.

I don't know how long I sat on that porch, I was caught in this chain of memory. Somehow I was aware that it was what I felt, what I resonated with emotionally at the end of this completed spell, which was important. Something had affected me over which I had no control, even if I didn't know what it was yet. Something in those woods.

**michael martin**

Michael Martin's fiction takes a
creative look at the perceptions of life.
Originally from Benton Harbor,
Michael now studies Child Psycology
in Kalamazoo, Michigan.  This is his
first published work.

*just desserts*

Mrs. Hackins supports Vigilantism at Coloma Elementary School, 1973.

Her drumming stride echoed among the construction paper turkeys who smiled trustingly as they posed next to grinning pilgrims sporting muskets and pumpkin pies. The Thanksgiving decorations colored the tiny hallways of the elementary school where Jean Hackins kept her vigil in her personal battle against the ignorance and disrespect that had been instilled into the children of all the inept, hippie parents that had invaded her town.

She had grown up here, met and married her husband here, bought her parent's house here. She wasn't about to ever allow her town to go to hell in a hand basket as a result of the influx of drugs and free love that had come with all the freaks and long hairs that could now be seen everywhere she went.

She casually adjusted her girdle as she passed Miss Evans' door. The younger first grade teacher was living with one of those weirdoes. And she was such a beautiful girl too. Mrs. Hackins felt sorry for the poor dear and the low self-esteem from which she must suffer. Why else would she want to degrade herself so by shacking up with one of those bead wearing, bongo playing, dope smoking hippies, rather than wait for a nice, respectable, real man to come along and marry her honestly? The moral shortcomings of that generation and culture group worried her.

They were even bold enough to come into her favorite store, Coast to Coast, that nice Mr. Badts owns. He knew how to treat a customer with questions. He always looked her in the eye as soon as she approached his counter and smiled genuinely so that she felt she was truly welcome there. Even when she was all the way over at the Hilltop Market, doing her grocery shopping, and they didn't have what she needed, if any of it could be found at Mr. Badts' store, she would make the trip.

At Carol Stubens' door Mrs. Hackins stopped and knocked firmly, but at a respectful volume. She liked Carol. Carol was close to her own age and possessed the same generational values as she did. They often comforted and supported each other over coffee and cigarettes in the teacher's lounge. They would share their harrowing experiences with the worst of the children under their care and bolstered each other's justifications for opinions and the dismay that they felt over the seemingly inevitable decline of moral character in society. She simply didn't know how she would live without Carol's support. Jean was sure that she would have torn all her hair out by now.

The door swung open and Carol Stubens' lean, soft face radiated into the hallway. Jean always wished she could do something for the poor dear's hair. It was so fine and difficult to work with. Styling and permanents were simply out of the question. They just wouldn't take. Curlers were of no use and the only way that her bangs could be controlled at all was to cut them straight across and short. The rest looked no better whether it was kept short or allowed to grow long and straight. She'd resolved, long ago, that there was nothing to be done about it. She didn't let any of her thoughts show in her face when she smiled sweetly and said;

"Hello Carol, dear. My little monsters are up from nap time and we'll be settled pretty soon now. That David Evans takes a bit longer than the rest of them to wind down, so I'd better hurry back. There's no telling what he'll get into in the few minutes that I'm gone. You bring your class down in about ten, okay? The piano teacher should be down with the piano soon. I heard him next door to me in Mr. Drake's classroom for nearly half an hour now, so... I've selected some nice traditional Thanksgiving songs for us to sing next to the teepee that you and I built in the play area. See you soon, dear."

With that she patted Mrs. Stubens on the wrist and turned herself down the hall towards her own classroom. Carol Stubens clucked her tongue on the roof of her mouth softly as she gently closed the door.

Mrs. Hackins was just considering what kind of nonsense she was sure that she would return to when a cry of pain jolted her eyes up from the odd discoloration in the broach that was pinned upon her huge bosom. It was a strange voice that cried out and was now wailing from her room. She didn't recognize the child. Normally she could tell who the victim was by their voice.

The assailant was almost always the same however. David Evans was the biggest and most merciless bully that she had observed in her thirty-one years of teaching there. He was nearly twice as big as any of the other children. He was overweight and always sloppily dressed. He often wore the same clothing for several days at a time and, although his hair was kept in a crew cut, the thick black strands of hair always appeared unwashed. His whole body was stout. Short, stubby fingers hung like miniature hams at the ends of his thick, round arms like the meat she once saw hanging in the Goldburg's butcher shop. His fingernails were always caked with dirt.

She was certain that the reason for all of David's social and hygienic problems were due to the fact that his parents were hippies. They must be. Those hippies were all spouting about free expression and allowing children to discover the world for themselves. There was no guidance any more. She stepped up her pace in order to get to the injured child more quickly while her mind conjured up images of streaming tears and feigned innocence.

Upon entering the room, Mrs. Hackins scanned the room for David's favorite targets. Stuart, Gregory, Scotty and Todd all appeared unmolested, although Stuart's big, blue eyes looked wild. Well then, where was David? He was not in his seat. Little Karen Hewitt had her soft, brown eyes trained intently on the vicinity of the play area. As her searching eyes raced dreadfully toward the teepee in the corner, Jean was certain that she would find it a burnt out shell or in a jumbled pile of rough timbers and symbolically adorned canvas. Saints be praised, it was all there and in one piece. David, however, was also there.

He sat, right leg cocked under him, half slumped in the old bean bag chair. David's large, round face was beat red and sweat covered. A wide fan of blood spread from his swelling lips to the base of his throat covering his chin completely. She almost laughed out loud.

He was staring in such disbelief at the blood smeared across the back of his hand that he appeared quite comical. Then she almost jumped for joy. Somebody had finally given that brat his just desserts. Who could it have been? She wondered this to herself as she heard herself distantly ask David what had happened to him. Her attention only focused on his response long enough for her to hear the name of her hero.

It was her turn to look wild-eyed as she shifted her gaze upon Stuart. More out of pleasant surprise than out of a reprimand did Jean lose her grip on stoicism when she cried out, "Stuart Arnold Collins!" Uh oh, she thought. She could see the fear in the thin boy's

face as he tried to melt into his desktop. He was
always such a good student. Stuey, as his friends
called him, was well-liked and very smart. He was
also quite wise for an eight year old. Jean had always
liked him. He didn't make any trouble, but he always
seemed to be the brunt of it. Of course, with David
Evans around, everybody was the recipient of some
sort of brutality. She was grateful that it was Stuart
that was going to be the champion of his peers. His
parents were not hippies. They were good, church
going Christians that emphasized manners and
education, as well as a healthy body. And, most
importantly, they emphasized discipline and responsi-
bility. She regained some, but not all of her voice
inflection as she had to ask the obvious question.

"Did you kick David in the mouth?"

The poor thing had been looking at David and she
began to doubt that he would be able to bring himself
to meet her gaze. A proper hero should be able to
feel confident in his actions.

*Come on. Come on Stuart, you can do it. Look at
me, please.*

She almost died when he was finally able to look
her in the eye and more nod than vocalize an, "Uh-
huh".

Thank you, lord.

This boy would grow up to be a real man. She
simply needed to display her approval in some way
now. These are the moments that Jean Hackins lived
for. This was an opportunity to see a child display the
benefits of good upbringing and the tutelage of an
outstanding teacher. She would have a part in the

building of a good character.

The Making of Heroes.

"Stuart Arnold Collins!" Mrs. Hackins called out sternly, looking straight at him from under high arching, crayon eyebrows. She looked ancient with her sagging cheeks that slid away from her long, narrow nose. Her half glasses hung by a chain upon her large, sloping chest. Her body, attired neatly in a sweater and skirt, was almost cylindrical from her breast on down.

Stuey looked uncomfortably down at his thin, pink hands where they rested atop his desk. He knew what was coming next. He knew what she was going to ask him. Slowly he drew his leaden gaze up and over to David Evans' bleeding mouth. The bigger, heavier boy sat on an orange, bean bag chair by the bookcase with large, wet streaks from the corners of his eyes back to his curly sideburns. Both his upper and lower lips were bloody and beginning to swell. When he grimaced in pain (Which now appeared more an attempt to milk every last bit of sympathy from the on-looking class than actual discomfort) there were evidences of blood on his teeth and gums as well. He sat there, belabored breathing pumping his barreled chest up and down quickly, causing the Incredible Hulk to leap wildly about the front of his fully stretched tee-shirt. Sweat glistened on his forehead and darted like tiny bunnies among the miniature forest of his crewcut hair. David supported himself with one arm upon the floor of the reading

area while the other hand extended before his fasci-
nated eyes where they marveled at his own red blood.
Stuey thought that perhaps David had always believed
his blood to be blue.

More of a flash across his mind than a conscious
thought in his scruffy blond, little head, Stuey recalled
the first time that he had encountered Sir David
Evans, bully, esquire.  He'd been playing marbles with
Scotty and Greg out on the playground of Coloma
Elementary School at recess.  They had their pit
heeled into the dirt and somebody had just shot when
David Evans came roaring by and gave a long, sweep-
ing kick with his dark blue Keds high tops at the
circle full of purees and cat's eyes.  Scotty even had a
steely in there too.  Sparkling glass and cloudy brown
dust blotted out their sun as the self proclaimed ruler
of the playground went bounding off across the yard
toward the swings.  Ironically, his laughter was quite
bubbly and pleasant to hear if your marbles hadn't just
been scattered from here to the equator.

The boys stood for a moment, grubby hands on
dusty, slim-waisted jeans, and then set about finding
and collecting their wayward combatants.  Greg
muttered something about Dunlop's Disease to Scotty
who added a remark about David's exposed butt crack
having an echo to it.  They all laughed secretly and
made booger-flicking gestures at David's stampeding
behind.

After that the boys were regular targets of spitballs,
peas, dirt clods, and unprovoked beatings.  Stuey
remembered one that was particularly vicious.  He'd
been playing "700" with some other boys , chewing

on the leather strings of his baseball mitt. The boy
with the bat and ball called out "Catch on the fly is
worth one hundred, one hoppers are fifty and doubles
are twenty five." At which point he threw the ball
straight up into the air, quickly grabbed the bat in
both hands where it rested on his shoulder and swung
at the descending sphere. The ball rose high into the
air and David Evans landed on the top of Stuey's back
driving him into the grass. Wham! Wham! Bam!
Pow! Just like on Batman, Stuey thought just before
the pain of the raining punches registered in his mind.
Then, David was gone, bounding, bubbling across the
playground toward the cement tunnels.

Back during the second or third week of young
Stuarts' first grade experience, he'd decided that he
didn't like it very much. Thus far he had had two bad
experiences since the school year had begun. On the
first day of school he'd gotten off the bus and was
wondering what to do next. The entire lawn in front
of the school was chaos. There were children running
and screaming everywhere. Some were even crying.
He had just realized that he didn't know where to go
and that he should find an adult to ask, when some
kid he had never seen before in his six and a half year
old life came out of no where, running at top speed,
and punched little Stuey right in the stomach. Stuart
had never felt so much pain. It was as if a bomb had
gone off in his tummy and the pressure didn't want to
come out but rather to suck the rest of him into it.
The next thing he knew he couldn't breath and the
bus driver in the open doorway was doing funny,
"round and round" dances above him. *Why?* That

was all Stuart could think to think. Nothing else would come to mind. *Why had this happened?*

Why had any of these things happened? Why had the boy in the bathroom yesterday yanked him away from the urinal where he was standing and looked at his pee-pee? He didn't have any idea, but he did know why he had done what he had just done to David Evans. He had wanted David to get away from him, to stop hurting him.

"Did you kick David in the mouth? Stuart?" His teacher drew him back.

He nodded, barely perceptibly, and answered. "Yes ma'am." His dark, blue eyes began to fill with tears. He knew that he should never hurt someone else. He'd learned in Sunday School class that he should always turn the other cheek. He knew that he had done wrong and that he deserved to be punished. At home he would probably get a swat or two with the heavy wooden paddle if he had made his little brother's mouth bleed. But what kind of punishment would he receive in the Principal's office?

Somehow the memory of the principal standing behind the microphone during the assembly last week and saying "You spell principal p-r-i-n-c-i-p-a-l because I am your pal." Wasn't at all reassuring at this time.

"David was biting Stuart on the leg, Mrs. Hackins." Stuart didn't notice who said that but he was grateful because his own tongue had frozen in his mouth.

"David is a big bully!" That was Corina Applegate, the girl who always tried to kiss Stuart

during indoor recess on rainy days that said that.
Maybe he would have to let her catch him next time
she tried. He dismissed the idea with a turn of the
stomach. Girls were icky, except for Danielle Jeffries,
whom Stuart decided was his girlfriend.

The entire classroom erupted in shouts of agreement. Stuey almost cried anyway, out of appreciation.

Mrs. Hackins thrust out her right hand index
finger lancing the air. "Good for you. It's about time
somebody taught that bully a lesson."

She turned her fearsome countenance upon the
disheveled antagonist saying, "You sir have gotten
your just desserts. Go to the office and see the nurse."
The room was silent as David rumbled to his feet and,
scowling at the floor, lumbered out of the room.

Mrs. Hackins turned to the chalkboard and wrote
in white chalk *2+3=*.

Stuart looked at the faces around him. Danielle
was scribbling in her notebook, Corey was blowing
him a kiss and grinning from ear to ear, and Greg,
who had caught Corey launching the kiss, was now
making pretty gestures at Stuey. He had a big, gapped
toothed smile and had his hand cupped just below his
hairline while he bobbed it up and down like he was
displaying the bounce that his shampoo gave to his
hair. Being a sort of hero never crossed Stuey's mind.
He thought that they were all heroes because they had
stood together when it had counted. Stuart had only
been the stone shot out of the sling that had brought
Goliath down. His classmates that day had been the
arm that wielded the sling.

## anne vandermolen

Anne Vandermolen's story has a
Raymond Carver style realism to it.
Nickey's Place is straightforward,
naked fiction.

Anne is from St. Joseph. She is the
mother of Bryan Vandermolen, who is
included in this volume.

## nickey's place

On Friday it is hot, over ninety all day. My husband comes into the bedroom. "I've got to stop at my mother's," he says. "Do you want me to pick you up afterward and go eat?"

It is late afternoon and I have given in to the heat. I am lying on the bed with a wet washcloth. I continue to sponge my face and arms. "Sure," I answer, sitting up. "I haven't been to see her in two weeks," I admit. "I better go with you."

"Get ready, then." He tells me, frowning, and leaves the room. I get up and decide not to change from my sleeveless shirt and walking shorts, although both are wrinkled. It's too hot, even to look for a pair of pants to cover my legs.

At his mother's house we sit, my husband on the

olive and peach colored sofa that needs a professional cleaning.  I settle into a green, plush chair that matches the one my mother-in-law is sitting in that faces the television, which she turns off as soon as we had enter.  She is eighty one and her walker rests beside her chair.  Six months ago she broke her hip, which is still mending.  She lives alone.

"I got a letter from Aunt Margie this morning," she says brightly, her news for the day.  She smiles at her son.

I look around.  The house is small.  Every framed photograph, knickknack, and pot of African violets is in its proper place, although several cobwebs have begun to gather dust above the living room drapes.

He asks about his aunt in a polite, respectful tone I do not hear him use elsewhere.

I don't say much, I am still feeling the heat.  She relates her difficulties with her stiffened hip, and her arthritic pain.  My husband listens, hands folded, eyes oblique.

Her air conditioner helps some, although I would have turned the thermostat colder.  It is almost seven o' clock, and part of my discomfort, I realize, is that I am hungry.

At last we leave, and I climb quickly into the truck, anxious to get to food.

"Where do you want to go?"  My husband asks.  I know, more or less, the choices.  "Anywhere."  I say, and I mean it.  The truck's cool air builds slowly.  It is going to be another beastly night, too hot to sleep.  We drive to Nickey's Place, a few blocks away.  My husband orders a steak plate special and I ask for a submarine sandwich, which is all I can manage, but I want it as soon as possible.

My husband orders a draft beer. I have an iced tea. We wait, silent. We have not eaten out together for many months. He comes here for breakfast on Saturdays.

We see Elliot come in and he sees us. Elliot sits down next to my husband and calls to our waitress by name, a young women in red shorts, and orders a draft beer. The two chat a moment. She is just back at work: her baby girl is three weeks old. She doesn't wear a wedding ring. She is about the age of my oldest daughter.

I continue to sit in the dark booth, cooling off, across from the two men. The paneled room, a long bar at one end, is filling. It is very cool and I am thankful. The two men discuss Saturday fishing plans. I finally ask, "How's Arlis?" I have not seen Elliot's wife in some time.

"She's home," he says, raising gray eyebrows and gazing at me through bifocals. He is an engineer, early retired. He returns his attention to my husband, telling him that his son will be coming up from the army base to fish with them. I mention the heat. "Is your house hot too?" I ask.

"No." Elliot says. "When I got home at three, I turned on the air for my good wife." He looks at me as if I needed to know this, that he is a help at home. His wife is a nurse

"When she comes home from work," he reports, "she heads right for the sofa, pulls on a blanket, and takes a nap."

He looks sideways at my husband.

"I ask her if she noticed I turned on the air and she just looks up and says, umm." Elliot grimaces, mimicking his wife's expression.

"Umm—umm?" he repeats with a twisted smile, raising his chin and lowering his eyelids. My husband chuckles.

I picture Arlis on the couch, half asleep, acknowledging her husband's question, but too tired to comprehend she is supposed to thank him for turning a dial. I know she gives him her paycheck every week.

I look at my husband. Then, I stare back at Elliot who is waiting for my response. I refuse to smile. I wonder what kind of face my husband makes when he is imitating something I have said to him. These are not kind men. In fact, I think, they would make terrible women. If they were women, I would not be their friend.

I see the young waitress approaching and I think of her hardships. She walks quickly, her arms laden with food.

I wonder what I am doing here.

## ione lake

Ione Lake currently lives in
Kalamazoo.  Her story exemplifies the
conservative Dutch influence in the
western Michigan area.

## *grandmother's garden*

My grandmother was a first generation Dutch American. She had a stern face with thin lips, a long nose, and hazel eyes covered with clear rimmed bifocals, all framed with tightly permed short white hair. She didn't smile much and had frown lines from the corners of her mouth down to the bottom of her chin and jowls on each side. I wouldn't call her fat because she had thin legs and arms but she seemed to have no waist. She always wore a dress with hankies wadded up in the pocket and sensible shoes.

To tell the truth, when I was little, I was afraid of her. She came from an era when children were expected to behave like little adults. She was not the demonstrative type and didn't show affection to me or anyone else as far as I knew. I was a rambunctious little girl brought up by permissive parents. I was also a late in life baby which made my mother old enough to be my grandmother, and made my grandmother ancient to me. I didn't know how to relate to her any more than she could relate to me.

Being much younger than my brothers and the last child in our family, I spent much more time at grandmother's than my brothers. I had to go with mother on Sundays to visit while they could stay home by themselves. I never spent time with my grandmother without my mother and I could tell that I only added to the tension between them. Although my mother looked like a younger version of my grandmother, with the same long nose, thin lips, hazel eyes and thick waist, they had nothing else in common. Mother wore contacts instead of glasses and had thick, chestnut colored hair worn into a chin-length bob. She always dressed casually but with style. The problem was my mother had too many kids to please my grandmother. Also, she didn't finish college, married the wrong man then divorced him, and didn't keep a clean enough house. Worst of all, we didn't even go to church.

Visiting grandmother wasn't so bad when she still had her house. It was a huge center-hall colonial where we had all kinds of fun places to play. Under the stairs in the basement was my mother's old play kitchen with a small table and chairs and a little white cupboard made by my grandfather when my mother was a girl. The cupboard was full of grandmother's discarded china including chipped cups, saucers, and an odd assortment of silverware. Also, there was a non-working hot plate, an old icebox, and a wash basin for a sink. I spent most of my time in that space playing house and having tea parties with mother's old dolls.

Sometimes, in nice weather, we would walk to Crane Park which was only a few blocks away. There were formal gardens featuring a long, grassy isle with flowers on each side and archways leading to more gardens. This was a popular spot for weddings and I loved to pretend that I was a bride walking down the isles while mother and grandmother would sit on a bench admiring the flowers.

A red, brick road divided the floral garden from an open area with tennis courts at the bottom. Just past the tennis courts there was a wooded area. It was an enchanting place with a stone path that my mother called "Lover's Lane". It lead to a roof over a cobble stone building built into a hill. The roof was like a balcony with raised sides, a perfect seat. My grand-mother told me the stone house was a witch's den and warned me never to go down to the bottom. The witch didn't like people going on her roof she said, but mother assured me that we were safe until dark because the witch would sleep all day. Grandmother also said that at night the witch would fly about the woods looking for naughty children for her midnight feast. From the wink in my mother's eye, I knew it was just a story but it was fun to play along.

The year I turned nine my grandfather died. My mother and her brother decided that the big, old house was too much for my grandmother to take care of and that she should move into a retirement home.

It was a very nice home and she had a charming apartment but it was all in one room. It was perfectly decorated with many breakable things. There was no dust, no crumbs on the kitchen floor, and never any dirty dishes in the sink. She also had a beautiful garden on the window seat in front of her bay window. She preferred flowering plants, especially bulb flowers like tulips, daffodils and hyacinth. My grandmother often said how she missed her garden at the old house, especially in the spring.

She didn't have room for the toys anymore so they were all sold at her moving sale. I asked for them but my mother said I already had too many toys and we didn't have room for any more. While visiting my grandmother, I was expected to take a book along or my own toys and play quietly. I'd try to enter into their conversation but they'd tell me to stop interrupting and entertain myself. Being only nine years old, that was next to impossible for me but I was still to young to be left alone at home.

When I turned twelve my mother finally said I didn't have to go with her to visit anymore which was as much a relief to my grandmother as it was to me. I didn't see much of my grandmother the next six years. Only during the holidays at our house and even then I stayed out of her way.

The year I turned eighteen things began to change. My mother said that my grandmother was getting forgetful and didn't always make sense. My mother and her brother also saw to it that grandmother sold her car. It took a lot of doing because my grandmother said that her car was the last piece of indepen-

dence she had, but they finally convinced her to stop
driving through guilt -saying that she was a menace to
everyone else on the road.

Mother remarried and started taking weekend
vacations with her new husband. My brothers had all
left home long ago and my mother decided I was old
enough to stay alone. My grandmother missed my
mother's visits and I, being grown up now, became a
substitute to her for my mother's company. Grandmother would call under the guise of seeing if I was
okay staying alone but, from the way she rambled on,
I could tell that she was just bored and lonely. She'd
invite me to her apartment for a home cooked meal
and I'd go only because I felt sorry for her.

The next spring vacation my mother decided to go
to Florida with her new husband and my grandmother called me and said, "Let's go on a picnic." It
had been a muddy, cold spring; not picnic weather at
all.

"Let's go out to eat, Dutch treat," I suggested. I
knew my grandmother wouldn't want to pay for my
meal and she wouldn't let me pay for hers but I didn't
want to have a picnic in the cold.

"Okay, but I have to run an errand after lunch."

"That'll be all right."

When I picked her up she was carrying a big,
plastic bag filled with something.

"What's in the bag?"

"You'll see," She said with a surprising twinkle in
her eye.

After lunch she directed me to drive to the park in
her old neighborhood and to park the car by the

woods.  It had changed a lot since I was a child.  The stone path that my mother called "Lover's Lane" was still there but the witch's den was gone -as was the balcony roof.  All that was left were the steps leading to it and a dirt hill, but the woods were as peaceful as ever.  Since the trees were bare, while we stood at the edge of the hill, we could see the whole town.

Then she got busy and pulled a small shovel out of her bag.  She instructed me to dig a hole and took a pot containing the remains of a plant out of the bag.

"What's that?"  I asked.

"These are my bulb plants.  I couldn't bear to throw the bulbs out so I decided to plant them here in the park."

"Aren't they supposed to be planted in the fall?"

"It doesn't matter.  Anyway I might not be around in the fall.  You know I'm going on eighty-seven."

As she planted her dozen or so plants she told me how she and my grandfather use to court in these same woods.  They use to take the trolley up to the top of Westnedge Hill to get here.  Long before they got married they decided they wanted to live in the neighborhood by Crane Park.

"Your Grandfather was very romantic.  He always gave me flowers and would write the most beautiful poetry.  He would recite it to me right here," she said pointing to where the balcony used to be.

I got a different picture of my grandmother and grandfather that day.

The rest of that summer I would visit my grandmother on Sundays, with or without my mother.  It wasn't out of pity anymore, I really enjoyed her company since I learned to see through her grouchy exterior. While taking walks she would teach me about gardening by identifying flowers and telling me how to care for them. We also spent time looking through old family photographs and discussing what life was like when she was young. During that time a friendship blossomed between us.

My grandmother was right about not being around to plant her bulbs that fall. She died suddenly in the late summer of a massive stroke. She left strict instructions that there was to be no funeral and she wanted to be cremated, because she "didn't want the undertaker to get any more of her hard earned money than necessary." She had one last wish though; on May 3rd, which would be her and my grandfather's anniversary, she wanted the whole family to have a picnic in the woods of Crane Park and scatter her ashes there.

Everyone but me thought this was a strange request. I remembered the day I helped her plant the bulbs in the woods and our conversation about grandfather romancing her there. I wondered if the flowers would even come up, but I didn't tell anyone about that day we spent together planting the bulbs.

May 3rd arrived and much to my surprise the whole family came. My uncle, aunts, cousins and all my brothers and their families, many of whom I hadn't seen for years.

There was another surprise when we arrived at the park. Instead of the dozen or so plants my grand-mother and I had planted last spring, there were more than a hundred bouquets of flowering plants scattering a rainbow of color through out the woods. There were red tulips, yellow daffodils, purple and pink hyacinths and many more flowers I couldn't identify. All those years in the retirement home before she lost her car, my grandmother must have gone out to the woods to plant her discarded bulbs. It was only in the last year when she didn't have her car that she had let me in on her secret.

I never told anyone, but now I always keep flowering plants in my house and, even though I have a garden, each spring I take some of the bulbs out to the woods and plant them. The only one who knows about it besides me is my grandmother, and it is our secret.

fact

**randall p. vande water**

Randall P. Vande Water is a lifelong journalist, writer and now, a publisher. He recently published four volumes of stories related to Holland, Michigan. "West Michigan Story" is one of the many funny stories that prove fact can be better than fiction.

*west michigan story*

On Decemeber 15th, 1888, under the *Holland City News* headlines of "Returned From the Tomb," John Bergman, who was "Supposed to have been murdered 13 years ago, Returns and a great mystery is cleared up," readers learned of the Fillmore Township man's strange saga.

Bergman had immigrated to this country from the Neitherlands in 1865. "This Bergman was a married man, and if there had not been a woman in the case, this tale would never have been written."

Sometime in 1873, Bergman left Holland and a few months later his wife received word that he had died in Chicago of smallpox. On the strength of this information she married Foppe Klooster, a Holland saloonkeeper. In 1875 Bergman returned.

"He was ignorant of his wife's doings in his absence, but finding her another man's wife, he decided to have nothing more to do with her, and an agreement was drawn up that he should relinquish all claims to his wife and depart and molest her no more. For this transaction he received the sum of $12," the *City News* reported.

When some of Bergman's former neighbors, "with whom he was not a favorite, owing to his methods in business affairs," learned of his return and were told that he had sold his wife, they "made up their minds to wreak vengence upon him." During a stormy, bitter cold night in February 1875 Bergman was waylaid by them and "Beaten in an unmerciful manner."

It was thought that Bergman had been murdered "as no trace of his whereabouts could be found. Great excitement prevailed, and the daily newspapers of Grand Rapids, Detroit, and Chicago contained long accounts of the murder." There were six assailants. They were arrested and taken to the Allegan County jail and charged with murder.

The woods were searched for his body. Bones of a skeleton were discovered a year or two later and were believed to be Bergman's. The six were tried for murder, but without sufficient evidence to hold them, they were convicted of assault and battery. The incident "faded from the minds of the people in this section, although many people believed that Bergman had been murdered," The *City News* said.

During the week of December 18, 1888, 13 years later, Bergman arrived back in Holland. The newspaper said the facts that had been reported "were revived and are now a chief topic of interest." Bergman was interviewed by the *City News* and "he told the following story in regard to his disappearance and his whereabouts during the last 13 years."

"He states that at the time he was assaulted, he managed to make his escape, five of his captors having left him in charge of one of their number, while they went in search of a rope with which to hang him. He made his way as rapidly as possible through the deep snow to Holland. He arrived there about 11 o'clock and took a sleeper on the midnight train to Chicago.

"On his arrival in that city he was unconscious and was taken to a hospital, where he remained in critical condition for five months. His injuries included a broken arm and shoulder blade, a deep gash on his head, and he was otherwise injured. After his recovery he left for the south, where he has remained since."

Bergman was "very bitter towards his assailants, and the object of his journey here is to prosecute them for damages," the newspaper reported. But nothing ever came of it.

# poetry

## audrianne hill

Audrianne Hill, resident of Holland, Michigan, has had works published in the Black River Syllabary. She is in a graduate program at Western Michigan University. Her works are visionary and thoughtful. She captures ideas through imagery, sight, and an unusual outlook.

## *the cape*

It was always the red and white check tablecloth
tied securely at the neck,
draped majestically over the shoulders.
When I ran, I'd imagine it floating behind me
high in the breeze, surging power through my body.
Against my small seven year old frame
it would hang below the ankles,
dragging in the dust of childhood saviors.
But I'd be ready to fight
the evils of the world.
Mom stopped looking for it eventually
as it lay each night beneath the blankets,
next to my side.
One never knew when a super hero would be called
to save the world.

## *the big c comes for the cowboy*

Hot and dusty.  No rain for weeks.
Good rattlesnake weather.
Vultures circle the sky knowing
what he knows.  He can't see it.
Feels it when it's too late.
The ache in his side screams the loud warning.
It's growing; glowing cryptonite green
attaching itself to the vulnerable spots
hidden beneath varnish leather skin
from too many high noons under the sun.
This isn't how it's supposed to be.
Antiseptic rooms, stainless steel scalpels.
The masked man is the enemy;
not dressed in surgical green trying to save your life.
There should be the thunder of hoof beats,
gun fire, smoke so thick you could choke.
He was meant to go out in a blaze of glory-
Butch Cassady and The Sundance Kid-
shooting it up in Bolivia and dying with your boots on.
Instead it's a fistful of dollars,
it's a fist full of pain pills, doctor's warnings,
and being poked and prodded
like branding day at the ranch.
"It's a bitch," he says,
and the only water for miles
wells up in his eyes.

## *the difference is all*

To get to you
in the spring, summer, and fall,
I drive through
five stop lights,
over the bridge,
around the lake and
two stop signs.

To get to you
in the winter,
I take a pleasant walk
over frozen water
speckled with shanties
hiding little men
like those in black forest clocks
waiting to come out and dance
when the hour strikes.

## *blessed are they...*

It just sat there flat as Sunday's newspaper
caught in the rain, then baked
to a fine wood one could flake away like phylo.
I didn't expect it to get up
and walk to the other side of the road.
It was too for that
Stuck and immovable
even a shovel might have difficulty
scraping the remains from the concrete griddle.
I have always felt sorry
for the chicken, and any other creature
for that matter, who failed to cross the road
and was left draped over the pavement
more exposed than a playboy centerfold with staples
strategically placed.
I cringe thinking
how they spent their last moments on earth,
"Should I go on?  Turn back?
Maybe I should duck and take my chances.
Maybe I should..."
My only prayer is they  went quickly,
feeling no pain following immediate impact;
that the god of creatures, perhaps my God,
took pity on their souls and the soul of the hit and run.

## ept on I-96

Tossed among the blades of burnt July
like the heat of the moment
that caused its results
a soul hovers waiting out the decision
between two hearts.
Its first notion of existence-
that pink streak across a space of white
is an albatross,
a three hundred fifty thousand dollar debt
that can be washed away
in a flood of saltwater.
With a "yes" or a "no"
its breath may cease to be
or give way to a dream for tomorrow.

# bonnie flaig

Bonnie Flaig is currently teaching at Kalamazoo Valley Community College. She has had works of hers previously published in various literary journals. "How to Feed Birds in Michigan" is a thoughtful piece that wakes up the conscience.

# *words for katie*

the months before you were born, I would sit eve-
nings on the deck, searching the woods for a glimpse
of your face. And you stayed always just beyond my
vision, appearing only once, briefly, as a doe at the
edge of the tree line. After that I was possessed with
imagining a thin ankle amid the twigs, the flick of a
white tail.

Now I see the same look on you, searching my face,
your tree line, for the words that tell you who you are,
what gifts you bring. We walk through the woods
together; on a margin of trees, honeysuckle bobs over
our heads. I make you a necklace of sweet white
clover, name you empress of my heart.

I have watched you consume words, devour them,
reshape them, claim them and hand them back. You
seek words in the green moss, your Golden Books, the
cat's fur, your daddy's anger, the row of perfect toes on
each of your feet.

Oh, my angel. What have you done, choosing me as
your mother? It frightens me to catch you examining
my face, the silent, desperate imploring of a traveler
with her interpreter in a terrifying new country.

I feel you study my profile now as I wash dishes at the
kitchen sink, puzzling, waiting to see what words go
with this scrubbing rinsing, and staring out the
window. Nothing. Nothing. Far out in the trees a
twig snaps. You begin to ponder the causes of silence.

## *how to feed birds in michigan*

Pour black oil sunflower seeds for the cardinals.
Remember your dead father and how he loved those
red birds.

Scoop thistle seed into the plastic column with eight
tiny feeding stations for the finches, purple, gold, and
house.

Bluejays will eat anything, heartless bandits,
and bully the others, too.

Fill the hummingbird feeder with nectar, but don't
expect to see one tonight.
Remember the dead one he showed you, emerald-
feathered body and insect wings.

Cut orange halves and impale them on nails for the
orioles, those blaze orange
harbingers with familiar five-note song.

Sit back now and watch. Think about all you've
reaped and all you've
failed to see. Forgive yourself.

# marsha meyer

Marsha Meyer is the Head of Adult Services at the Portage District Library, in Portage, Michigan. She has had works published in *Poems Ate Your Eyes* and *Encore Magazine*. She attended Western Michigan University.

## *the barn*

Facing non prevailing wind north,
settling into its slope
both doors on ground level,

muddy, crinkled windows twinkling
reflectively like the eyeglasses of a wise,
crook-of-a-smile professor,

pumping, churning, spewing, bearing,
status and shrine, womb and catacomb,
brimming with bone, blood, fur and fiber,

it is the fulcrum,
balancing existence worn fragile
from snapping cold winters,
wet through the skin springs,
dry as dust summers.

It is coming full circle
home.

*milwood*

Milwood is a Sears Roebuck catalog
of no nonsense
brown and beige bungalows
sweet-as icing dollhouses,
neat-as-a-pin starters
trimmed in billiard ball shrubs
and needle point perfect petunias.
A tiny brick cottage bedecked
with a white Persian
and primly preened window boxes
looks like the third little pigs house
rock solid and full of safe karma.

Silver maples frame the street like filigree
on the ivory pages of a favorite story
expressionless, within pursed lips,
But sometimes,
within the murmuring night shadows
or the morning's paradream haze,
clues peak out from a droopy spirea
or a dribble of yellow light through the blind.

At dusk, a bronze patina
washes even the shadows
in cool browns.
Pocket smells of spaghetti
and grilled steak
waft in and out.
Voices flicker pale
behind amber screens,

and cat silhouettes
settle onto window sills.

Like a worn,
hung on the line smelling quilt,
the neighborhood nestles
around me,
while the rest of the world
slips on by.

## *responsibility*

You chose staghorn sumac
and seven sisters clicking against
bubbled bedroom windows
at mid afternoon

I chose two leased vans,
payroll deduction
and a monthly writing group.

You live in the country.
I moved to the country.

You plant herbs
to Brandenburg's Concerto No. 5.
I balance the checkbook, file nails
and eat Cheeros out of the box
at stoplights

You go without a phone
when the egg count is down.
I dream of hiring Mrs. Doubtfire,
for life.

I layer each night's leftovers
into tiny, color coded
Tupperware boxes.
You toss them into your garden,
for next year.

When taxes are due,

you plant iris bulbs.

Winter solstice
you send me a hawk feather
and entwine your poetry into mine.
I mail you a down jacket
I find at a garage sale.

Habit of years, you whisper,
arranging sweetpea in my hair,
is stronger than life itself.

## *mineral springs*

In the corrugated greenness
surrounding Deighton,
sits Mineral Springs.
By day shit-brown peeling plywood
etched in dripping globs of caulk
cracked neon and dead beer cans

By night...
a flee market jewel in the middle of Starry Night.
A pleasure palace
lined with red, white, and blue half ton
Ford pickups.
Pipe fitters in tight liquid denim and cowboy boots
gravel-haired beef and mashed potatoes
none of the pasta shit, farmers,
leggy, fat-haired, Virginia Slim smoking starlets
straight from Marion High School Homecoming
Court to Tustin Corner Gas and Go
enter the show.

At Mineral Springs
rum and coke and pitchers of Bud
alchemize up one dusty row down the next
furrow lives into smooth as ice pool mavericks,
slick as leather, don't cross me, babycakes madonnas,
and roughsawn whiskey voiced country crooners.

At Mineral Springs the script is black and white,
whittled clean.
Learn the tune and the words are free.

Sutters Home chardonnay
twist off intimacy...
sweet and easy.

Mineral Springs...where everything flows, everyone
glows.

## barbara spring

Barbara Spring is from Grand Haven, Michigan. She has had works published in *Michigan Out-of-Doors*, *The Grand Haven Tribune*, *Grand Valley Review*, and *The Grand Rapids Press* and many more.

## great yin mother

We're trolling for trolls or silver salmon
for anything below our quivering lines
we hold taut and eager.  The dark yin mother dances
over small salmon and gives us one small king leaping.
Rocking to and fro on her thighs
the motor mutters low
At Palisades, a spent fuel rod
a slowly decaying plutonium tomb
perches on the dune.

Once a toddler seeing Lake Michigan
for the first time dreamily called it "milk."
Great milk mother tumbling with
fossils of ancient whales
and corals, the ribs of sunken ships where fish dream.
As she loves to do, the yin mother plays crest and
trough-her sweetwater laughter laps us, and as we tumble
in her lap her laughter splashes shore away-Sand dunes
collapse the sunny wooded dunes where we once played
crumble before yin's fluid grace.  The droll mother
juggles bones, trees, ancient roof beams, plutonium
while we forget to turn out the lights.

## lake michigan aubade

Mist rises, March morning
a song bird's longing shears moist air,
drifts from thickets.
From empty porches of summer homes
wind chimes play, hollow medodious shards of clay.
And the lake never ceases sounds in March:
ice chunks chink, shards break and break
against the shore.
Waves dash ice against troll caves of ice
and break ice feet.
Mist rises from green briars
where wild birds braid their songs
through tangled skeins
and the blood that rushes through my veins
echoes
the waves
on shore.

## *refuge*

The beach seagull lovely
surf sand painting the shore
I slept on the sand
washed in wave sounds
and awoke to find myself covered
with ladybugs.

These bright orange insects sought
refuge in me
as if I were driftwood
sand
or a tree.

## marc carls

Marc Carls is from Centreville, Michigan. He was a senior in High School at the time this was written. He currently attends Western Michigan University. This is his first published work.

## *clichés*

Lips as red as a rose;
as if all roses are red.
It should be lips as red
as a stop sign, or a fire truck.
And eyes that sparkle like stars:
Stars look like little white specks to me.
I want to hear someone say:
his/her eyes sparkled like a chrome grill
off a '57 chevy sitting in the sun.
And pearly white teeth?
Pearls are dull and some are black.
Teeth should be as bright as
a welder's torch.
Let's turn up the hydraulics and raise our standards.

# julie stotz

Julie Stotz's poetry is a blend of
realism and dreams.  Julie's poems are
everyday stories beautifully told.  She
captures amazing amounts in her
works, leaving thought and wonder in
her wake.

## *the sandals*

Tonight, I am saddened by the way the sun just
slipped
away without color.  Maybe it's because of the
weather-
brisk, and no one has much energy.  Someone left
a pair of sandals in the hall, a few feet away from my
door.
Brown straps, scarred, soft-my size.  They could be
mine,
except it's winter and cold snow soaks wool socks.
I want to slip my naked toes inside them, to feel
leather
on my skin.  I want to walk with sandals in the snow.

This dry snow, the kind I catch with my tongue, falls
loosely;
I mean to say it doesn't fall down, exactly.
It rides the wind, defies gravity.  It's elusive:
coming and going all day between patches of sun.

## *pale reflections*

I, with my back to the source, consider
moonlight's tendency to cast shadows,
its pale cool reflections.

There's something serene in the dark
silence of my inverted body,
something to remember.

Lake water. Mid-summer. Blue
bodies rise and arch above depth. You,
undaunted by moonlight,

lie flat on the sand,
run your fingers through sand.

I study your movement
and guess meaning in rendered lines:
*blue arcs over black,*

which I suppose is true.

Your body does not rest in sand.
It is a white scar that fades
in the first few moments of sleep.

You are silver slipping into silver
And that is all I understand.

## *curiosity*

it may take a lifetime,
but someday I'm going to figure out
why I can't stop looking at snow
as it falls, often gently,
as it lays, always quietly,
and, sometimes, as its frozen shards cut my face.

*winter songs*

A man at a counter leans
on his right foot, bends
his waist slightly to the left
and right as his hips move
to some rhythm in his head.
I try to make out the words
as they form on his lips
because I desire the sound.
Because I've been looking for a song,
a voice that rises from my stomach
and fills my mouth.

When I was little,
I made tunnels in snow drifts
and sat for hours in blue-gray spaces
that sucked the echo out of noise.
There was no mistaking myself.
Even the rasp of my breath
became so obvious that to leave that world
was a kind of rebirth.

Now, I'm afraid of silence like that.
I fill empty spaces with unnatural tones
and sighs.  Not the music I remember,
not the music I think speaks
for what I know, which is the same
as what I don't know:
why pure white caves melt away.

On the sidewalk, a hundred faces

look at their feet. I watch the marks
they leave behind in the snow. Empty
fountains fill with the heavy notes
of piped-in Christmas music,
songs heard too often to be recognized.

## the unlocking (in michigan, the extra season between winter and spring)

1.

Rain falls into my shampooed hair, and I am taking out the trash,
breaking down cardboard boxes, soggy cardboard boxes.

I seek the amazing.

My gray T-shirt freckles.

I don't want to be some rambling woman with a shopping cart, stuck
in the infinite thaw, feeling the burn from frozen to lukewarm.

2.

When you live in a small apartment,
you notice the sound the refrigerator makes.
It is a chain smoker telling a long story you've already heard twice.

Hint:  When seeking the amazing,
environment matters.

Plain truth.

You can't be too cold, too distracted,

too shaded, too illuminated, too alone,
too occupied, too passive,
or too comfortable.

Things happen while you are adjusting

3.

On my way home, I drive by the barber shop on
Burdick street. There is one big glass window in the
front, a frame for what happens inside. The same
man sits each day, except Sundays and Mondays, in
his barber's chair, sometimes reading a newspaper,
sometimes watching me out the window, watching me
pass like I watch him sit. Sometimes he's behind the
body of some other older man-They're always old
men-looking over his shoulder while he reads the
newspaper, or while he watches out the window,
watching me pass. Everybody watches everybody else,
making up stories about existence outside their own.
We should thank anonymous sources for giving us
importance.

4.

I wanted to be at the beach looking into the ice-cube
lake from the snow
drift at the end of the pier. Instead, I spent 45 minutes in the shower, warm

water ticking the top of my head, flattening my hair
against the side of my face,

unable to move, entranced by the ugliness of my own
image, knowing

I should move, scrubbing myself with soap.  Lather
and lather and lather.
At least the smell was soothing, and the water over my
face cleaned something away,

or did it hide something?

5.

I know this is bad-It's, at least, unhealthy-
the way I linger and contemplate,

but I can't accept spring's assurance.

Nature's buds are peppy cheerleaders that say, *buck up!*
While my mind is still a bare-boned tree
and nothing seems amazing.

## christine phillips

Christine Phillips lives in St. Joseph,
Michigan.  She has been published in
*Blossom Review, Great Lakes Review,*
and *Shoreline Voices.*  Her poems
capture the essencial Michigan themes
of a past long gone.

*silver beach*

Roller coaster shrieks,
The Whip and Comet...
Lana Turner in a bathing suit
for a nickel.
Jane Mansfield, Marilyn Monroe
photos dropped from a slick machine
in the penny arcade.

One night, the alewives' stench
was so bad, we closed the
windows in 90 degrees.
Watched man take
first steps on the moon
on the old black and white.

Steaming hot
in the morning,
I'd walk the pier
and build a castle
or bury myself in the sand.

The water was clear.
I'd slide little feet
over algae stones
and dive to swift minnows
to become a mermaid.

### sand rabbit on lake street (for mrs. hekert)

Some nights, we'd rock
on the wide swing,
old German women.
Lighthouse beacon shining
and the steady motion
as they gossiped
into the night.

Walking each other home
arms entwined at elbows
like endless braids.
We'd walk the alleys.
I would look up to a star
and whisper "twinkle, twinkle
little star..." and wish for a prince.
Swift as a storm cloud over the lake-
childhood became a sand drift.

# *hour glass stand (for david and rachel)*

Through wide windows at the pier,
below the boulevard park-
the autumn expanse
of the beach,
children,
sifting through
their own sand rabbit dreams.

## mary louise westbrook

Mary Louise Westbrook is from Muir, Michigan. Her poems in this collection follow the season's changes and capture the thrill of each. Written in a spacific style, she defines Michigan in her words.

## *blizzard!*

Raised trumpets from the bosom of the air!
    Announce the blizzard, driving o'er the fields,
    the windward dagger, winter fiercely wields.
    Emblazoned in its strident, wayward sheath,
Such smooth confection, blows the vestal wreath!
    In purest vestments, its tapestry toss'd,
    Aristry of ornamaental glaze, emboss'd,
Its cover, more abundant than the fair.

The tyrant of the north displays its rage,
    As stark confinement lends majestic still;
    As tho' blithe spirits sent these gails forth.
Flow onward, in vain glory, the wondrous sage,
    The winding beast, its fury e'vr shrill!
Blow!  Blow, this master of the savage north!

## *a tinge of spring*

return again, oh dear departed sun!
   'Tis long since past your warm, hypnotic spell.
   Beneath the dour earth, the scarabs dwell.
   Deplete the snowy mound the bitter chill.
I long to hear the throstle gayly trill!
   Awake to morning, scout birds of the snow!
   'Midst murmurings of bees in gentle prose,
'Til quarries of the savage cold are none!

Oh remnants of the winter, hid thy face!
   Abate the tides of wind-lashed veils, nigh!
   For overhead are tidings of the spring-
Evolving from profusions of thy grace!
   The gown of teeming, patient life will sigh,
Until the waves of warmth and fallows ring!

## *late summer*

Ev'rywhere the light of some deep ember peers,
    Amidst the silent and pastorial ground.
    Where torrid heat and breath of the day surround
    The meadows.  Soon dispossessed of lengthened
grass,
As smolder of the flame have turned them to brass.
    Where rooks will glide upon the faintest breeze,
    And prayerful skies of golden scallops tease,
As declination on the shallows, nears.

Solitude decends as daylight blurs,
    'Tween tidals of the windward shifts and scants,
    Above the stratus veils, the shavings die,
In faint remembrance, whilst the current stirs,
    The primal vestige of the cricket's chants,
Will close this sacred passage with a sigh.

## *the turning leaf*

Its faintest shadows filled the languid days.
    A wisp.  Behold, the grace with which it clings!
    As tho' held aloft by alabaster wings.
    Amidst these heights, this merely translucent weft,
Resisted wind's intimidating theft.
    Or purched in noontide's unrelenting heat,
    And bathed in fireglow at evening's feet,
This crimson scroll, amidst the golden maze.

Prepared to join its brothers in their sleep.
    Asunder cast, by time's resistless stroke,
    The Turning Leaf, a fair and distant blush,
Wafts downward, etched in tide's eternal creep.
    The dormant and immortal forest cloak,
In somnolence, invest a hidden hush.

## kerry l. hansen

Kerry Hansen grew up in Coloma, Michigan. She graduated from Western Michigan University. Much of her work reflects time spent in Coloma and the negatives of growing up in a small town atmosphere. Kerry brings a truth and simplicity to her writing that sticks to the soul.

## in an ailing hometown

We try to poison our young here

Some shrivel like brittle fallen leaves
And scuttle down Paw Paw Street
Past the old dark bars and white churches
To settle like wet mulch in trailer parks
And crumble behind glass convenience store counters

Our tourist attractions include summer orchards
Where brown hands pull ripe peaches from
Spindly armed trees, to be dropped
Into baskets held by round brown babies
We don't keep those young either

A few of the ambitious ones manage to escape
They empty from the high school in spring
Then climb into dented cars and roll away
to colleges that promise the cures
For the maladies of a small sickly town

But you'd rather hear of our young mothers
Who make fat babies in clouds of sweet smoke
They raise them up in run-down cottages
Then slowly beat them down with their
Bruised words, whiskey fists, and hot shotguns

Yes we've always poisoned our young here
So they'll be sure to stay and grow ancient
Even if it takes only a few short years
To choke down the bitter taste of hope
And suffocate in the leftover moldy silence.

*valley*

There's a ditch full of them,
lily of the man-made valley.
A tractor tire or a deer
carcass can flatten, easily-
linen bells and flat woven leaves
I'd pick a fistful for Mothers
on their many days, and pick
my teeth with a stem or a neck

but she hates to see children in a ditch.
So I just watched instead, instead
of taking a scythe or my canines
to them. Lilies all bow down when
I run clumsy paw over top.

And they shiver. Because even if.
Maybe they can see grasshoppers
coupling, but they couldn't look up,
even if.

I walked all the way out to the edge
here at the corner of the stop sign
and the lake. They would have been
bending, but not begging, even if.
If I were a waitress in Mackinac
and a pink skirt, they'd never have seen
me. I visited the rotting white tail
on the straight highway, so it seemed
fair. To lie down in the wet ditch
I took off my boots, and to breathe the
lilies I had to walk far away from the stench.

## somewhere i grew up

anywhere but Sunday, air heavy and gray
the soggy brunch between morning, and after
anywhere but vinyl passenger seats, wet windshields,
   the staticky ache of AM football
a green-shag sitting room, slipcovers, and dark
   paneling-no one allowed to touch
anywhere, anywhere, but a church stuffed with
sausages,
   wool coats and born again halos

I think I'm anyone
   but that dead town
somewhere wrapped in eternal November
I think I'm anywhere but Sunday,
   but still breathing its thick air

## joseph a. fester

Originally from Benton Harbor,
Joseph Fester now resides in Grand
Rapids, Michigan. He is the editor of
FUSE Magazine. Joseph's works are a
clip-art collection of feelings and
thoughts. His writing carries with it
an under current of promise and
strength.

## *fine summer dresses*

all of these girls
in their fine summer dresses
all of my life spent in chase

all of these people
with their different obsessions
all of our lives in vain

## *september*

september
a year has come and gone
       slipped in and out and through our hands
       before we were given half a chance
            to ask the favor
       september

september
seven burning reminders
       of the flame that we once shared
       a love you use to care so much for
            forgotten... remember?
       september

september
love was not an option
       my heart so young and unexplored
       your world so ready for a lord and king
            shining armor
       september

september
summer breathing her last
       soon a far gone collection
       with no hope of resurrection
            memories forever
       september

## *she*

She came to me softly
singing songs of sweet sorrow
saying, "Sometimes it's better
to be awf'lly sad"

Slowly she spoke
soothing my soul
so this is the angel
who saved the poor lad

Sing away

## another day

woke up this morning
not a worry in my head
i had no place to go
forever said goodbye
to the job that wore a suit and tie
but at least i awoke

in our haste
to ever succeed
simplicities are foregone, forgotten
then the wealth
by which we wage our worth
becomes a cloud to veil the sun

bless those dear Jesus
who've no time to rest
all the roses pass them by
come the evening
when their life has rushed before their eyes
they've only time to die

woke up this morning
not a worry in my head
i'd found a peace of heart
refreshed by the rest
my next journey i begin
with a single step start

## quite sure

i'm really quite sure that its a good thing
that i've gotten myself into
but i'm not so sure it's had exactly
the same effect on you

i'm really quite sure my life is changing
for the better, for the good
but the way you carry your lips, your eyes
makes me wonder if i should

i'm not so sure

i'm really quite sure the door is op'ning
to a new celestial shore
a bigger, brighter world where maybe
you don't fit no more

i'm really quite sure that this could be
only just the start
of the tearing, thrashing, beating, smashing
reformation of my heart

yeah, i think i'm sure

i'm really quite sure that you're dying
at least you're dying to me
was it that you were my sin
now lost through focusing

i'm really quite sure that i'm done now
with the chains i wore for you
broken now, on the ground
i'm free, i'm clean, i'm sure

really quite sure

## bryan vandermolen

Bryan Vandermolen's early death left
those who knew him with memories,
and those who didn't, with his poetry.
A strange, simple style that makes the
reader smile and think, Bryan had
achieved a plateau few can achieve.

*mara*

a stark golden skin washes over the top of
this Lake Michigan mist-
a blanket of sunshine brilliance way above
May fog churning so palpably that
sifted currents move through
just a half block ahead.

The far bend in my lake shore drive
is sleepwalking into purgatory-
a tight red edge of the lighthouse is buffeted by gray
its geometry turned to stomach humming
fog horn bellows.

An iron train bridge is
a skeleton sinking in the featureless
stew of this day.
The mallards are lost, calling out their way-
squealing gulls and knocking sailboat sides.

Car lights open up ahead of the
mossy silhouettes,
the wet tire rush.
St. Joseph is huddled under this nest of gray.

But the sun spares nothing on a high billowing
surface,
while way down the oaks lose their leafy resolution-
A screen is stretched between pairs of everything.
Milk mist drifts where each thing parted
from another,

each of these ten thousand things.

A chop of pier side wave checks briefly loose,
and wind moved obscurity grabs in between.

*service poem*

Easiest thing in the world's when
a flame follows down the match
or an ice cube turns to water-
a thing's already started, and it's going on.
You drop some money in the box-
write a letter to your governor.

## *performance haiku*

Exhale deeply, and
pretend it's the last time you
will ever do this.

## *sidewalk piece*

-Find a sidewalk which is at least moderately crowded

-Choose a fixed point before walking towards it.

-As you pass the chosen point begin seeking eye contact with each passerby.  Smile pleasantly.

The piece is finished when someone smiles at you.

**dave wilson**

David Wilson is from Grand Haven,
Michigan.  He catches a simple
moment in "January" and makes the
reader aware of its importance and
lack of importance at the same time.

# *january (on lake michigan)*

The light of the capsizing sun strikes Lake Michigan
with
startling urgency and
a colorful delicacy,
Purples and oranges dance off these juxtaposed
waves of ice.
I focus my dazzled eyes upon these waves,
they appear to be frozen in time.
Without warning, nature's ice sculptures begin to
uncoil, and breathe.
They untangle themselves and emerge from their
huddled position
like butterflies breaking free of cocoons.
All at once, the winged ice figures crash forcefully into
one
another
to form an exotic castle of
purple and orange joy.
I blink my eyes, and the lake falls back
to sleep.

## todd koebke

Todd Koebke is from Portage, Michigan. Originally from Flint and a graduate of Western Michigan University, Todd's Bukowski-like realism paints a picture worth looking at.

## *fall into me*

Icy blue stare brought me into her like midnight tide
There was a breeze that ran through me with painted
nails
My steps were quick
Avoiding the sharp rocks that can pierce bare skin
In the distance the old light house stood tall
passing its beacon across the blackness
Proud to protect the whores that ran the sea
If I let her get close she could bring me to my knees
Makes a man feel weak
But I want to be ready for what you do
So into the night we ride
Two lovers
Eyes closed and head back the coldness hits with the
swiftness of a seasoned pro
I arch and she peaks
We fall together
Crashing into us
Crashing into night
With my eyes to the sky I can only see sprays of white
light
that fade away with me
Good night my sweet.

## *little boy lies*

Walking down this sidewalk in steps of trouble and
truth
An infested town
People all around me
Looking, staring
All wondering what could possibly be wrong
I blankly push on in search of some little café and
locate one on the East side of town
Trendy little place
Walk in to find colorless faces
reading and discussing
discussing and reading
Different books, magazines, and others
Simply enough just to fill the void
Nobody understands comfortable silence anymore
I pull out a Harrison that I happen to have in my
backpack
I want to be one of them you know
attract less attention that way
Blend in with the grayness of the room
I light a cigarette and pretend to read
I am strategically placed in front of the window
just so I could see all the little angels that pass by
My eyes wonder upon every shaking ass in tight blue
jeans
I prefer the arousal of a fully dressed woman to that of
naked flesh most of the time
There is something so much more erotic about the
unknown
I ponder this as the young girl working the counter

comes to my table
hey you're that local poet guy she says
can I get you anything, anything at all
An espresso,
cappuccino
mocha,
triple latté, light creme, double caramel, extra cinna-
mon, chocolate sprinkle...
Black, black, black I come in with quick
Would you like to read for us? she says
The people here would love you. she says
I just smile
looking her up and down
wondering just how pink it is.

## *crazy wisdom*

The bus came late today as it does when promptness
is required
Westnedge always slows everything down, especially
on steamy Saturdays
The heat is already working itself upon me
I feel a little sick to my stomach
I'm thinking about you and that makes me wonder
who is pulling my strings
I juggle the heat and you in my head for a while and
come up with both
"Jingle Bells, Jingle Bells..."
Thrown back, abusively I might add, to reality I look
around to confront the intruder.
"Hey boy." Comes from what I think at one point
might have been a strong man.  He
is covered in worn paperbags and shoestrings.  His
hands are thick, like a construction worker, some hard
labor at least.  With black teeth he screams,
"What's the matter, boy?  Looking at your future."
He laughs a horrible laugh like he's telling the truth
"Shut the hell up, old man"
There you go again.  Disrespect, disrespect, disre-
spect."
"Why should I respect you?"
"Why shouldn't you?"
"Sit with me," He says in a soft, non-harming way.
I do, not sure why, just do.
"Do you know what truth means?" he says.
"Truth to what?"
"To life. To love. To yourself."

"Yeah, I guess."

"No you don't" He shoots back quick, "You never guessed. I bet you never even questioned truth."

"Nobody uses it. Nobody thinks of it and nobody dares to try it."

"Crazy," I whisper under my breath.

"That's it," he screams, "Crazy wisdom hides all the answers. We all have fears, mental trials that screen the naked face. No one wants to answer to who they are. It runs as deep as the marrow. The shining lights we all hold are hidden in the attic 'cause we're afraid they aren't as bright outside as they are in. No one dares to become truth. It's a catch twenty-two son, a wild ride. In the search for meaning, I'm just a user's guide. Ha ha."

"Right on time," he says as the number three to West Main pulls up.

"Merry Christmas," he tells everyone as he steps up on the bus.

The driver flashes him a Wehaveawinnerhere look.

The doors shut and the metal monster lurches away slowly with the flow of traffic.

As I watch it go, I can see the old man making his way to the back of the bus.

He takes the last seat and turns toward the window. With a tip of his hat and a black smile he is gone.

I get up and leave as if I had

finally come to my senses.

## tara barry

Tara Barry grew up in Portage, Michigan and graduated from The University of Michigan. "None of the works are titled for a reason: I don't like titles. I think they can bias a reader's interpretation; I'd rather have a reader enter the poem freely and ultimately title it for him/herself."

## *untitled*

Bobby Blue-eyes has a little-boy laugh,
        Jingling pockets, and a candy stash.
He wears white cotton t-shirts and cuffed-up jeans:
        He hasn't changed much since 1918.

Thank God.

Bobby Blue-eyes carries a comb, and a handkerchief,
        Walks with a shuffle, smiles like a thief.
He sings "The Jelly-Roll Blues" with a smoke-cracked
voice,
        And would tuck me in every night if he had
the choice.

Thank God.

Bobby Blue-eyes bleeds with the faintest scratch,
        Has high blood pressure, and a glycerine
patch.
But he still my strongest hero,
still my truth that never lies,
Still the steel in my foundation,
and the source of my blue eyes.


Thank God.

## *untitled*

I blame the Romantics;
They have greatly deceived me.


There I sat waiting for the Heavens to Sing,
                    the Earth to Shake,
                    the Sun to Set in colors more
                    vivid than Imagination-

And all the while missing the smaller glories of love.

As if it wasn't true without Thunderous applause;
As if it wasn't right without Divine proclamation.

Romantics, you have led me astray;
You tainted my expectations with such silly raptures
That I very nearly missed the simple joy
Of resting my head on his shoulder.

Unforgivable.

And yet...

If only the Rose Buds would Bloom upon hearing his
name...

*untitled*

I am driving Home today,
Through mile after mile of slope and shadow,
Chased by nothing,
Save myself.

I am alone today,
But for this stranger at my side:
Somewhat me, somewhat distant.
She urges me to check my
Rearview Mirrors,
Looking for the layers of skin
I shed
With every mile marker of past,
Until -at last -I feel
Smooth...
Baby skin, daughter skin,
Lying within.

Then, around the bend,
A sinking feeling-
Something I've forgotten.

Something I've forgotten.

I drive with faltering resolve,
One thought repeating and repeating:
Please...
Someone familiar
Be There!
...Waiting for me.

Then, around the bend,
I know -Yes, Know!-
I must Drive
Many more miles before
I am Home.

## *editor's note*

Now, it's my turn.

My life is divided into houses. More to the truth they haven't always been houses. There have, in fact, been some really rat-trap type places that actually, when all things are considered, should have had the landlords locked-up.

All of these places have had strange things in common. For example, I lived at 53 Washington Street in Nantucket, Massachusetts, 533 Abbott Road in East Lansing, and, the two apartments I have had are both #3 (this has nothing to do with 3 a.m. publishing, by the way). The occurance of 3 is not the only similarity.

I lived at 53 Washington with my good friend Scott Hecklik, to whom I owe my love of books. We shared a room for a summer in Nantucket and drank too much, worked damn hard, and occasionally tried to find Richard Nixon's face in the clouds. To get to this room you had to walk down a hall that had uneven floors in front of the bathroom -bad news on the Fourth of July celebration when Scott found himself in the shower the next morning and not in his bed.

Since that summer, I made a habit of disappearing for the summer only to reappear back in East Lansing in the fall. Some of the locals that found me in their bars were places like Beaver Island, England, Malaga, Spain, and Prague.

Sometimes the living conditions were worse than others.

On Beaver Island, the apartment next to ours caught fire a week before we were supposed to move in. We didn't move in on time and they never fixed the place next door. The burnt-out shell left a smell on our clothes as if we were chain smokers (we were). The worst part of it was that the local teenagers looking for a place to smoke or shack up with someone always found their way to the burnt-out apartment. We woke up many mornings to the sound of parents looking for their teenagers.

When I lived in room #3 in Commonwealth Hall, at the University of London, I found my room overlooking a courtyard which was also looked over by a group of children from Italy. They had apparently learned the music to the "Mission Impossible" theme song just days before sharing that courtyard with me. I went to sleep many nights to that theme song being belted out with a slight Italian swing to it.

My point is this. My current apartmant, apartment #3 in an old brick building in East Lansing, Michigan, I will look back on as the apartment where I completed putting together *I-94*. It is a goal I am extremely proud of. Ask me and I'll tell you.

While I look back at some other 3's, I'll remember friends and beer and badly stained carpet, but when I look back at this apartment, I'll think of what you are holding right now. Thank you.

*-Brett Van Emst*
*Apt. #3*
*East Lansing, MI*
*Just shy of 3 a.m.*

I-94
a collection of southwest
michigan writers

edited by
brett van emst

to order additional copies,
to find out about up and
coming events, or to get on our
mailing list

write to:

3 a.m. publishing
p.o. box 6309
east lansing, mi 48826

# 3 a.m. publishing

east lansing • portage

# Copyright Information